Access Your Online Resources

The *Staying Well Facilitator's Guide* is accompanied by a number of printable online materials, designed to ensure this resource best suits your needs.

Go to https://resourcecentre.routledge.com/speechmark and click on the cover of this book.

Answer the questions prompt using your copy of the book to gain access to the online content.

T0372196

"Claire Holmes has crafted a masterpiece. It should be a gift from every school to every single student aged 7–12 who will see a friend move away at the end of the year. Too often the adults' attention goes to the students and families packing their bags and boxes. This book fills a long overdue gap in the hearts and minds of the stayers. We have long suspected that the unresolved losses associated with being 'a stayer' can impact the ability of these students to make and maintain long-term emotional bonds with others. Claire's book addresses this gap, with a storehouse of accessible tricks and tools. Do not be mistaken by the playfulness of her approach: it is based on sound psychological science mixing mindfulness, cognitive therapy, and polyvagal theory. This book will help kids stay well and fully reap the benefits of a life where change happens. We owe Claire Holmes a debt of gratitude for writing it."

Dr. Douglas W. Ota, *author of* Safe Passage: How mobility affects people & what international schools should do about it. *Founder, Safe Passage Across Networks (SPAN), psychologist, presenter, consultant, researcher.*

"*Staying Well* is a true gem for kids facing difficult times. The activity book's creative approach makes it not just a book but a canvas for young minds to explore their emotions and questions and build their resilience. It's a practical guide that fosters self-reflection and personal growth whilst providing a platform for nurture and support at a difficult time. The *Facilitator's Guide* is a reassuring companion for adults, equipping them with all the tools and insights to be the supportive rock a child needs during times of loss and change. These books are engaging and incredibly valuable, providing children and their supporting adults with the resources they need to navigate life's changes and challenges. A must-have for anyone supporting a child whose friend is moving away."

Dr. Pooky Knightsmith, *world-renowned expert on mental health, author, keynote speaker and advisor.*

Staying Well Facilitator's Guide

Coping when a friend moves away is hard. The *Staying Well Facilitator's Guide* contains guidance notes, prompts, and bonus material that helps the facilitator bring out the best experience for the child using the *Staying Well Activity Book*. This practical guide can be used to support one child or a group of children by parents, class teachers, learning support teachers, and counsellors. Support material is included to help the lead-adult feel confident in their delivery and in responding to questions related to the discussion.

Every page in the *Staying Well Activity Book* has a corresponding page in the *Staying Well Facilitator's Guide* for the user to refer to when delivering the material, which features:

- A page rationale which touches on the theory behind the activity.
- A visual of the corresponding page.
- Materials needed.
- How to set the scene.
- How to complete the activity.
- Facilitator's top tips.
- How to close the activity.
- Possible extension activities.

Grounded in wellbeing and transition research, this guide is an invaluable companion to the *Staying Well Activity Book*, helping a lead-adult support children whose best friend is moving away.

Claire Holmes is a school counsellor; her approach is trauma-informed and strength-based, empowering others to access their inner wisdom and knowing. As a mindfulness teacher, she weaves meditation into her work, alongside expressive therapies, and solution-focused interventions. She delights in spending time in the great outdoors and is a Nature and Forest Therapy Guide in training. She's passionate about positive transitions, having lived and worked in Singapore for over two decades, and understands first-hand what it means to be 'a stayer'. She is the author of the *Moving On* series and is delighted to add the *Staying Well* books to her collection.

This book is part of a set –

Book 1: *Staying Well Activity Book* is jam-packed full of strategies and creative activities to help 'the stayer' reflect on how they feel, appreciate their friendship, and build a coping repertoire.

Book 2: *Staying Well Facilitator's Guide* offers guidance notes and prompts to help bring out the best experience for the child and is designed to help the lead-adult feel confident in their delivery and in responding to any questions. It contains key points to consider, examples of 'what you could say', and explains the theory behind the activities.

Staying Well Facilitator's Guide

How to Support Children whose Best Friend is Leaving

Claire Holmes

Routledge
Taylor & Francis Group

LONDON AND NEW YORK

Cover credit: Hana Holmes (design) and Lisa Dynan (illustrator)

First published 2025
by Routledge
4 Park Square, Milton Park, Abingdon, Oxon OX14 4RN

and by Routledge
605 Third Avenue, New York, NY 10158

Routledge is an imprint of the Taylor & Francis Group, an informa business

British Library Cataloguing-in-Publication Data
A catalogue record for this book is available from the British Library

ISBN: 978-1-032-70459-3 (pbk)
ISBN: 978-1-032-70461-6 (ebk)

DOI: 10.4324/9781032704616

This book is part of the *Staying Well* set, ISBN: 9781032663548

Typeset in Helvetica Neue LT Std
by KnowledgeWorks Global Ltd.

Dedication

This book is dedicated to my two children, Hana and Ben. They have been 'stayers' far too often over the years. May you both grow resilience and perspective from your experiences, laugh, love, and be happy.

Acknowledgments

Heartfelt thanks to my husband Chris for always encouraging me in my hairbrained endeavours. Appreciation goes out to my close friends who have moved away, who taught me how to be 'the stayer', and helped me understand the value of true friendship, you know who you are. Thanks to my school counselling colleagues, past and present, much of your inspiration is in these pages, you are all awesome. Lastly to my ever-wise counselling supervisor, Helen Wilson, you are my guru.

Contents

The Staying Well Activity Book

Page title	Page number in the *Staying Well Activity Book*	Corresponding Page in the *Staying Well Facilitator's Guide*
Welcome!	1	1
Change happens.	2	4
What stays the same and what changes?	3	6
Friendship facts.	4	8
Magic memories: highlight reel.	5	10
Staying Well takes TRUST.	6	13
Wellbeing scales.	7	15
How do I cope well?	8	17
Saying encouraging things to myself.	9	19
Rainbow breathing.	10	22
Taking my pencil for a walk.	11	24
My circle of support.	12	27
The magic of vitamin N (N = NATURE).	13	30
Creative connections.	14	35
What my body tells me.	15	37
Draw feelings out.	16	39
Feeling focus.	17	43
Gratitude banner.	18	45
Purposeful planning.	19	48
Goodbye Card for my friend.	20	50
A message from my friend.	21	52
Cool connections.	22	54
What's in and out of my control?	23	57
Appreciating strengths.	24	60
Star strengths.	25	62

How to use the *Staying Well Facilitator's Guide*

The material within the *Staying Well Facilitator's Guide* is differentiated for supporting one child or a group of children. Some guidance is explicitly directed at parents, and some directed towards teachers/therapists. The lead-adult is encouraged to choose the pace of facilitation, to deliver the pages in a different order, not to guide some pages, or to leave some pages out altogether. They may decide to present the material differently than suggested or change/remove parts of the activities or guidance. This way, the material can be tailored to the needs of the target individual child/group. The facilitator may ask the children to complete some pages in their own time, with or without an adult helping. Throughout the guide, suggested scripts for the facilitator are highlighted in italics, these can be tweaked or changed to fit with how the lead-adult would usually articulate. In essence, this is a guide, the lead-adult is invited to use it with discernment and flexibility. Each facilitator will bring their own flair and style to delivery. It is intentional that there is no approximation of time needed to complete each page, facilitators are best placed to decide timings based on the children they are working with and how deeply they want to dive into the material. Some pages will have a lighter touch than others. The lead-adult may encourage children to decorate their page as fully as they wish, adding their own style. This increases investment, for this reason, coloured pencils/pens are added to the material needed list, even though they may not be explicitly needed for completing the page.

Author's notes – supporting 'the stayer'

Support is often extended to 'leavers' and 'arrivers'. However, those left behind when their friend departs, are, for the most part, not considered. Dr. Douglas W. Ota can be credited with bringing attention the often-forgotten plight of 'the stayer'. The *Staying Well Activity Book* and the *Staying Well Facilitator's Guide* are dedicated to supporting those children whose best friend is leaving. The departing friend will most likely leave a big gap in 'the stayer's' world and the idea of a long-distance friendship can seem scary and difficult to adjust to. However, with the right support, children, and their friendships can weather change and they'll learn and grow in the process.

I'd like to share some things that, I hope, the adults in the lives of those children left behind will find helpful in support of their 'stayer'-

Parents/guardians, do model being calm and steady about the change. Our children are not programmed to be calmer than we are. They take their lead from how we deal with situations. Be calm yourself, even if you are not sure how it is going to turn out for your child.

Talk to your child about their friend moving at a time when *you* feel calm. Think about what you can do you to reduce your own stress levels to be helpful.

Do let your 'stayer' know that it is okay to be experiencing all sorts of emotions. Whatever they are feeling about their friend leaving is okay. If you are supporting a young person to cope with this change, encourage them to come and chat to you when they feel they need to. Keep the door open for those conversations. Making yourself available to chat will help reduce their anxiety. Listen more than you talk. Avoid the temptation to tell them not to worry. This minimises their experience and may deter them from sharing with you. It might even increase their anxiety. Instead, normalise, validate, and empathise whatever emotions they are feeling about their friend going. Encourage them to share their feelings with other supportive people in their lives too.

what is normalizing, validating, and empathising?

When you **normalise**, you let 'the stayer' know that it is normal to feel this way, so, you might say "It's totally normal feel confused about this."

When you **validate**, you let 'the stayer' know they are heard and understood. You might say something like "Gosh, that sounds tough, I can really hear how you are considering all the options and it's confusing for you."

When you **empathise**, you let 'the stayer' know you can see their perspective and might say "I can really sense your worry here about getting it right, I get that."

There is no typical response in terms of how 'the stayer' might feel. They may be sad or angry more often, this is normal. Knowing they will not see their friend as much is painful. They might even feel jealous that their friend might make new friends or worry that they will be forgotten. They may fear that they will be alone when their friend goes and that they will never finding another close friend like them. They may catastrophise about it and start to imagine how awful it is going to be without their friend. Notice when 'the stayer' seems low and encourage them to do something to lift their mood. Help them think about what this might be, at a time when they are feeling okay, pages 7–8 in the *Staying Well Activity Book* help with this. Coping strategies vary from child to child. Some may like to do something musical; others will be artistic; others might like to get up and move and some might like to stay still; meditating or reading. Remind the child that whilst it feels devastating and there is no doubt that the friendship will change, it does not mean that it will have to end. They will still be there for each other, and with effort, their friendship will continue, but in a different way.

One over-arching thing to note is that throughout this process of transition relationships are paramount. The bedrock of being able to support fully is a kind, understanding and ideally playful relationship. If you are a parent, spending time with your child, as a whole family and just the two of you, will help them to feel safe and supported. Use the power of distraction at this challenging time, do fun things, laugh, and let them know when you notice their strengths in action. Encourage them to remain active as exercise breaks down stress hormones. They might need time alone, find a balance between connecting and letting them have space. If you are teacher or counsellor, raise awareness of this with 'the stayer's' parent/s or guardian, check in with 'the stayer' regularly to monitor wellbeing. Parents, guardians, and teachers, if you feel that the child's daily functioning is being impacted by the move do seek extra support.

The key to a child 'staying well' after their friend leaves is helping them prepare in advance. Being intentional about managing this transition ensures things are not forgotten. The TRUST acronym, provides the nuts and bolts of 'staying well.' A checklist of sorts, to enable a smooth transition (see image on the right). It's important that 'stayers' understand the value of considering these five things as part of their 'staying well' plan.

'Staying Well' takes **T-R-U-S-T**

T – Take care of you

R – Remain in contact

U – Unload feelings

S – Say goodbye

T – Take opportunities

A close friend leaving is an unwanted and often unanticipated change for children. This happening may lead children to feel a loss of control even for the most flexible and adaptable. One way you can help with this is to offer lots of choices. Choice is empowering. Being given choices helps children feel in control in times of change. Try empowering the child with choices, with small decisions that impact them. For example, what to do as a family activity, meal planning and the like. Teachers and therapists should weave in as much choice as possible in their interactions with 'the stayer' too.

Building a 'attitude of gratitude' can be a good way to lift mood. Parents/guardians, this might be done as a daily family activity, or your child might like to list a few things each day before bed they feel thankful for. Teachers and therapists may weave this attitude into sessions. Page 18 in the *Staying Well Activity Book* hones in on this.

Help 'the stayer' remember a time when they faced a significant change and successfully managed it, despite not being sure how it was going to turn out. You might like to ask them something like 'Do you remember how scared you were when it was time to move to a new school?' Ask your child what they did then that helped them get through it, you may be able to draw out more coping strategies. Ask them what they do now to help themselves feel better in times of challenge. Encourage them to engage in whatever is helpful for them to cope well. Share your own stories of coping in times of change and, parents, remember to do things that help you relax at this stressful time too.

It is okay not to have all the answers to every question or to not know how every detail will play out. Be honest saying 'I'm not sure how it's going to go either, but I'm sure you'll cope.' It is very important to tell your child that they *can* cope with their friend moving. You might ask older children, 'Given how you feel, what's your plan?' This plants the seed that they are capable and you trust they will figure it out. Ask them about their strengths and which ones are going to help them most, page 24 of the *Staying Well Activity Book* helps with this. Resist the urge to 'fix' the problem for your child by 'rescuing' them or advice-giving. This is a teachable moment for you and your child.

After the off, help 'the stayer' remember and get organised for their departed friend's birthdays and other celebrations, support them in sending their best wishes. Talk about the next time they may be able to see each other, if that's possible. Do encourage time spent both on and offline with new or remaining friends. Help them think of ways to widen their social circle. Perhaps there are clubs they could join to meet others with similar interests? Do remember they will not recover straight away from this loss, they may well be upset, a bit down and angry for a little while. No matter how much planning goes into the final goodbye it's going to be tough and there will most likely be tears. This is another opportunity to normalise, validate and empathise.

Times of change provide much learning both for 'the stayer' and those supporting them. Parents/guardians, trust in your own and your child's abilities to get through this, celebrate the learning. Teachers and therapists know your support for your 'stayer' is deeply valuable. Remember, times of challenge and change build resilience, wisdom, and strength.

I hope you have a much fun facilitating the *Staying Well Activity Book* as I had creating it. May your journey through the pages alongside your 'stayer' be fruitful, creative, and bold.

Staying Well Activity Book

Page title: Welcome!

Page no: 1.

Page rationale: This page welcomes the reader, stating the book's purpose and what to expect from the *Staying Well Activity Book*. The text introduces the concept of being 'a stayer' and includes a hopeful quote at the bottom. The child begins to take ownership of their process by writing their name and sharing a little about themselves on their page.

Page visual:

Welcome!

You've been given this activity book because your best friend is leaving. It's hard being 'the stayer' who is left behind. It's a book that helps you share how you feel and learn ways to cope with change. Each page has a different activity. You'll get creative by drawing, colouring, writing, and making things. The last page is a 'brain dump' page for you to plan anything you need to.

This book belongs to _____

My friend's name who is leaving is _____

They are moving to _____

> **Goodbyes may not be forever; they may not be the end;**
> **they simply mean farewell until you meet again.**

1

Materials needed: Each child needs: pen, pencil, rubber, sharpener, coloured pens/pencils, activity book. Optional: timer.

Setting the scene: You may say, '*Welcome. You've been given this* Staying Well Activity Book *because your close friend is leaving. As you move through the pages, you will learn more about being 'the stayer' which means the person who is left behind. You'll explore what* *this means to you, your friendship, your feelings and learn some important things you can do to 'stay well' after your friend has moved. We are going to have some fun completing the pages, I'm here to help and answer any questions. If you are ready to get creative, let's begin…'*

Completing the activity:

1) Read the paragraph on the page or ask the child/ren to read it themselves.
2) Ask the child/ren to fill in the gaps on the page, using the lines provided.
3) If you are a parent supporting your child, you may choose to move to the next page in the *Staying Well Activity Book* now. You may say, *'Let's move to the next page to begin our journey through the book.'* Teachers/therapists you may choose to move onto step 4).
4) If you are supporting one child, ask them to share with you what's written on their page. Ask them a few questions about their friend, how long they have known them, where they met, what sort of things they do together. You may say, *'Thanks for sharing a little about your friend, you'll be thinking more about how special your friendship is and how to stay connected with your friend as we move through this book together.'* If you are working with a group, you may invite the children to pair up, share their name, the name of their friend who is leaving and where they are moving to. If time allows you may like to go around the group, asking each child to introduce their partner, sharing their partner's name, the partner's friend's name and where their friend's partner is moving to.

Facilitator's top tip: If a child becomes upset by sharing this information, do normalise and validate. You might say, *'It's so tough being the stayer, it's normal to feel sad when your friend leaves. I can see that this is a really hard time for you, you'll probably be feeling all sorts of different emotions and it's all a bit confusing. Working through this activity book will help you cope with this change in the best way for you and I'll be here each step of the way.'*

Closure: You may say, *'Thank you for sharing, I am really looking forward to hearing more as we move through this activity book together. Let's turn over to the next page to continue our journey through the pages.'*

Extension activity: If time allows, you may like to offer a rapport building activity of your choice. One idea that works with one child or a group is to set a timer for one minute, pair up the children if you are in a group, be the child's partner if there is only one. Decide who will go first, in one minute the first person tells the other as many facts about themselves as they can, the other person needs to listen carefully.

Facilitator's top tip: If you are in a big group, you may choose to demonstrate this first by sharing for one minute about yourself.

After one minute the child who was the listener shares three facts they heard with their partner. If time permits you can invite students to share with the wider group what they heard too. Swap over and repeat.

***

Page title: Change happens.

Page no: 2.

Page rationale: This page seeks to normalise change, to help 'the stayer' understand that transition is a normal part of life. The child is invited to recall and reflect on a previous transition. Remembering times of change and what was helpful increases confidence about the current situation and the child's sense of efficacy to 'stay well.'

Page visual:

Change happens.

Change is a normal part of life; nothing stays the same forever. Perhaps you have moved from one school to another, moved house, or from one sports team to another. Your friend leaving is another big change, and it will take time to adjust.

Fill in the gaps... a change I remember is:

from _____ to _____

Draw something above to go with this change.
Write something below that helped you cope:

2

Materials needed: Each child needs: pen, pencil, rubber, sharpener, coloured pens/pencils, activity book.

Setting the scene: You may say, '*This page helps to realise that change is a normal part of life. The good news is that human beings have the inbuilt ability to cope with change. Your friend leaving is a big change. Remembering a time when you moved from one thing to another may remind you of what helped last time.*'

Completing the activity:

1) You might like to read the paragraph at the top of the page aloud or invite the child/ren to read it silently to themselves.
2) You may say, '*Choose a time you moved from one thing to another and write what it was on the lines on the page. Draw something to represent your transition in the box and write something below your drawing that helped you.*'

Facilitator's top tip: Some children might need help with choosing a transition, if so, revisit the ideas in the paragraph or, if you are in a group setting, hear from others what they have chosen.

3) When the child/ren have completed their page ask them to share as little or as much as they would like. You might like to do this in pairs if you are in a group setting.

Closure: You may say, '*Now we know that change is part of life, let's look more carefully at the change that's happening with your friend moving away and consider what changes and what stays the same on the next page*' OR if you are concluding for the session, '*Next time we return to this activity book, we'll consider what changes and what stays the same with your friend moving away.*'

***

Page title: What stays the same and what changes?

Page no: 3.

Page rationale: This page helps 'the stayer' acknowledge change and accept what is. Recognition that some things will remain the same, even though their friend is leaving, helps feel grounded and steady.

Page visual:

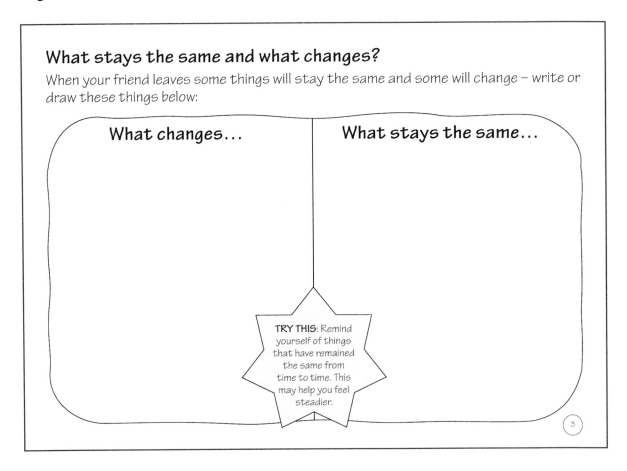

Materials needed: Each child needs: pen, pencil, rubber, sharpener, coloured pens/pencils, activity book. Optional: timer.

Setting the scene: You may say, '*This page helps you recognise things that stay the same and things that will be different when your friend leaves. At times like this, it might feel that everything is going to change but it's important to acknowledge things that will remain constant even with your friend's departure. Knowing this can help you feel steadier.*'

Completing the activity:

1) You may say, *'Let's begin by thinking about things that will change once your friend goes. I'm going to give you some time to write or draw these things on the left-hand side of the page.'*
2) If you are supporting one child, invite them to share some or all of the things they have recorded. If you are supporting a group, you may invite popcorn sharing (invite children to share their answers aloud in random order).

Facilitator's top tip: In a group setting, highlight similarities and differences between popcorn sharing examples.

Facilitator's top tip: Resist the urge to try to fix the problem, listen and repeat back to the child what they have shared, notice and acknowledge.

3) You may say, *'Next, let's think about things that will stay the same, these may be things in your environment, routines, family activities, or things that you'll keep doing even though your friend has moved. I'm going to give you some time to write or draw these things on the right-hand side of the page.'*
4) If you are supporting one child, invite them to share some, or all the things they have recorded. If you are supporting a group, you may like to pair up the children. Invite them to share with their partner things that will stay the same. You may like to put a time limit on this and invite them to swap over so that they each get a chance to share. Find a way for the children to share their examples with the wider group.

Facilitator's top tip: Again, listen for similarities and differences. Look for opportunities to highlight that even though their friend is leaving, it's still possible to carry on with things they enjoy. Emphasise this will help them cope better at this time of change.

5) Bring attention to the star in the bottom, middle of the page. You may like to invite one of the children to read this to the group or to you, if you are supporting one child. Let them know that noticing things that are constant can help them feel steadier.

Closure: Be curious to what the child/ren have learned whilst completing this page. Highlight not everything is changing, it's a period of change for sure, but some things will stay the same.

Extension activity: Invite the child/ren to continue to notice things that will remain the same and over the next few days. You may consider checking-in with them next time you support them with the activity book to see what they noticed. They may like to add these things to their 'What stays the same' list.

***

Page title: Friendship facts.

Page no: 4.

Page rationale: This page helps to process change by focusing on the friendship, bringing appreciation and acceptance. The focus on things that the child likes about their friend and themselves seeds the way for recognising and acknowledging strengths later in the *Staying Well Activity Book.*

Page visual:

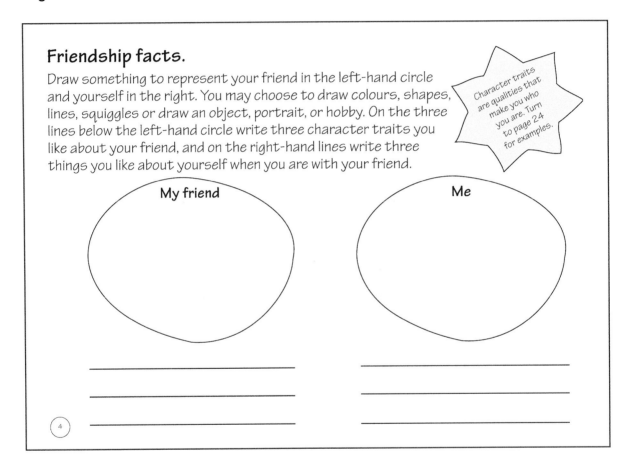

Materials needed: Each child needs: pen, pencil, rubber, sharpener, coloured pens/pencils, activity book. Optional: music/additional art materials for decorating circles.

Setting the scene: You may say, *'This page helps you appreciate your special friend, yourself and your friendship.'*

Completing the activity:

1) You may say, '*Let's get started by using creativity. Draw something to represent your friend in the left-hand circle and yourself in the right. It doesn't have to be a masterpiece, it can simply be colours, shapes, lines, and/or squiggles, it might be a portrait or a hobby that each of you likes. There is no right or wrong. I'll give you some time to do this now.*'

Facilitator's top tip: Direct the child/ren to the materials provided, offer a variety of choices. You may choose to play some relaxing music whilst the child/ren are being creative with their circles.

2) Guide the child/ren to consider, character traits, qualities that make their friend who they are. Bring attention to the grey star on the top-right of their page. Give some examples like, brave, funny, helpful, thoughtful. You may like to invite the children to turn to page 24 of the *Staying Well Activity Book* to see some more examples.

3) Invite the child/ren to add three of their chosen character traits on the three lines below the circle that represents their friend.

4) You may say, '*Often when we have a good friend, we are the best version of ourselves when we are with them. Now, add three character traits you show your friend when you are together, underneath the circle that represents you.*'

5) If time allows, you may invite the child/ren to remember and share about a time when they and their friend were being the best version of each other, together. Invite sharing of where they were, what they were doing and how that felt. This can be done 1–1 if you are working with one child, in a group setting they can share with each other in pairs, each getting an opportunity to share.

Closure: You may say, '*This page has been about appreciating both your friend and yourself, for who you are when you are together and things are going well. On the next page, we'll think more about special times the two of you have spent together.*'

***

Page title: Magic memories: highlight reel.

Page no: 5.

Page rationale: This page celebrates positive times in the friendship to hold dear. There is a Magic Memory Technique shared to cement happy friendship moments before and after the friend's departure.

Page visual:

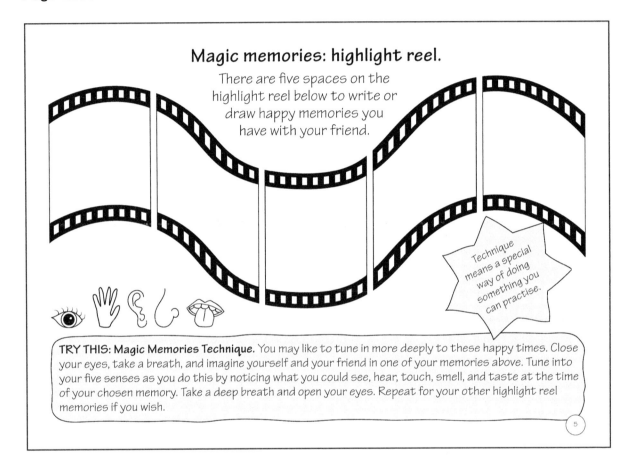

Materials needed: Each child needs: pen, pencil, rubber, sharpener, coloured pens/pencils, activity book. Optional: bell, scissors, scrap paper, glue, and a way to print images.

Setting the scene: You may say, '*This page features a highlight reel that has spaces for you to recall and record five magic memories of good times with your friend. When you've done that, we are going to try a technique to help you tune in deeply to these happy times which may help lift your mood at times of struggle.*'

Facilitator's top tip: If the child/ren ask what technique means, direct them to the star on their page and read it out to them or ask them to read it aloud.

Completing the activity:

1) Ask the child/ren to think of five happy times with their friend. Invite them to make a list of these either on the page, on scrap paper or use the brain-dump page (page 33).
2) Next, invite the child/ren to choose a way to record their five memories, one in each box. You may say, *'Choose one of your magic memories from your list. Find a way to draw this in one of the squares in your highlight reel. When you've done this, add the four other magic memories to the highlight reel squares, one by one.'*

Facilitator's top tip: If time and resources allow, you may consider assisting the child/ren to print out photographs to add to their highlight reel.

3) When the reel/s are full, if you are working with one child, invite them to share as little or as much as they would like with you about each one, or their favourite, if time is short. In a group setting find a way for them to share with each other, either in pairs or move around the group one by one, inviting them to share their favourite memory. If you'd like to get the children up and moving, ask them to choose their favourite memory, get out of their seat and move around the room. Sound a bell for them to stop and pair up with someone to tell their memory to, using their highlight reel if they like, make sure they both get a chance to share. Sound the bell again, ask them to move around the room, sound the bell for them to stop and find a different person to share with. Repeat this as many times as appropriate.

Facilitator's top tip: You may like to add a bit of fun as they are moving around the room, challenging them to take giant steps, to be as small as possible, to be like an elephant or other animal, etc.

4) If you've had them up and moving, ask them to find their seat again.
5) Read them through the Magic Memories Technique at the bottom of the page.
6) Be curious about how they feel after the exercise. You may like to ask them, what they noticed about the exercise and how they felt afterwards.

Facilitator's top tip: Most children will say that they feel warm or joyful after this exercise, but some may share that they feel sad as they realise how special their time with their friend has been. Let the child/ren know there is no right or wrong way to feel, and all feelings are messengers, letting us know what is important.

Closure: You may say, '*Thank you for exploring your magic memories, using your highlight reel. I encourage you to practice the technique we tried together, at a time when you feel okay. Your mind needs to practice doing this for a few goes before you can use this technique to lift your mood in a time of challenge.*'

***

Page title: Staying Well takes TRUST.

Page no: 6.

Page rationale: This page introduces the acronym TRUST, a checklist of sorts that provides the nuts and bolts of 'staying well'.

Page visual:

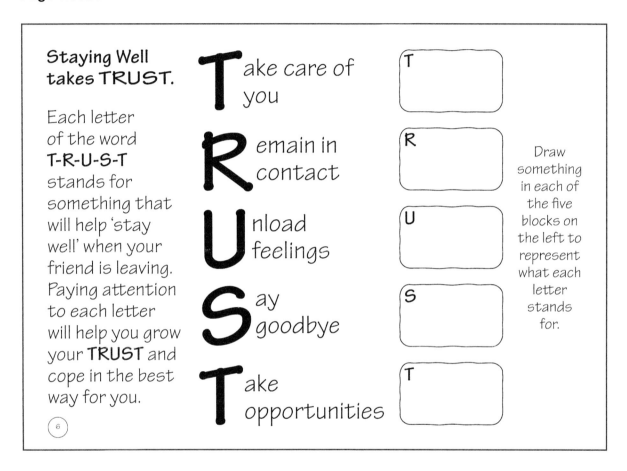

Materials needed: Each child needs: pen, pencil, rubber, sharpener, coloured pens/pencils, activity book.

Setting the scene: You may say, *'Staying well' takes trust that things will work out okay. Each letter of the word TRUST stands for something that will help you get through this tricky time in the best way possible. Paying attention to each letter will enable you to grow your TRUST. Let's explore this a bit more…'*

Completing the activity:

1) You may say, '*The T is for Take Care of you – this is about doing things to lift your mood and cope well.*'

2) You may say, '*The R stands for Remain in Contact – this is about making plans to stay connected with your friend.*'

3) You may say, '*The U is for Unload Feelings – this is about sharing how you feel.*'

4) You may say, '*The S stands for Say Goodbye– which helps you focus on farewells.*'

5) You may say, '*The T stands for Take Opportunities – this letter helps you find ways to build connection.*'

6) Ask the child/ren to close their books and recall what each of the five letters of TRUST stands for.

7) Ask the child/ren to open their books to page six again and fill in the five blocks on the right with a doodle that represents each of the letters, their drawings can look like something specific or be abstract using colours, shapes, lines, and/or squiggles.

8) If you are supporting one child, you might like to ask the child to talk you through what they are drawing for each of the blocks and invite them to explain why. If you are in a group setting, you may invite the children to share with the person next to them as they are drawing.

Closure: You may say, *"In order to 'stay well' you'll need to pay attention to each of these five blocks. This will help you cope with your friend leaving; the next few pages look at each of the five letters of* TRUST *to help you plan how to do this."*

Extension Activity: Movement break – If you are in a group setting, divide the children into five groups. Give each group one letter: one group gets T. Another group gets R and so on. Ask group members to join to make their letter shape using their bodies.

***

Page title: Wellbeing scales.

Page no: 7.

Page rationale: This page begins the letter T-section of the TRUST acronym, 'Take care of you' and begins the journey through coping strategies. It raises awareness that participation in activities that bring joy boosts wellbeing. It encourages 'the stayer' to choose to engage in their chosen joyful activities to lift their mood. Wellbeing is defined, a theme that weaves its way through the *Staying Well Activity Book*.

Page visual:

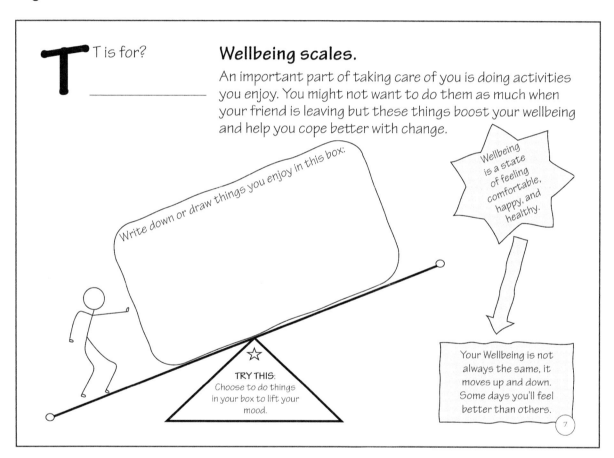

Materials needed: Each child needs: pen, pencil, rubber, sharpener, coloured pens/pencils, activity book.

Setting the scene: You may say, *'When your friend leaves, it's a confusing time. You might be feeling fed up and not as motivated to do your favourite things. It's easy to forget about taking care of you at a time like this but doing so will help you cope. The next few pages explore some ideas of how to do this.'*

Completing the activity:

1) Begin by inviting the child/ren to fill in the **T is for** _____ on their page. You may say, *'We arrive at our first letter of letter of* TRUST. *Can you remember what T stands for? (Elicit from the child/ren: Take Care of You.')*

2) Bring the child/ren's attention to the grey star on the page and either read the definition of wellbeing within the star to them or invite them to read it silently to themselves. In a group setting, one child may read it to the group. Ask the child/ren to follow the grey arrow to the box, bottom-right and read this too.

3) You may say, *'This page is unique to you, no two pages will look the same. Think about things you enjoy, examples might include doing something sporty, something in nature, something artistic, writing, talking with someone or something musical. What do you love to do? Write or draw these things in the box on this page.'*

4) Find a way for the child/ren to share something from their box. You may like to do this verbally or in a charades-type activity, asking the child/ren to mime one of their chosen activities for you or others to guess.

Facilitator's top tip: If you are in a group setting and some children finish before others, ask those who have finished to put a star by the things that would lift their mood most.

Closure: You may say, *"Your friend leaving is a tricky time, and most people, at a time like this, do less of the things they enjoy. But, remember the better you take care of you the more likely you are to 'stay well.'"*

***

Page title: How do I cope well?

Page no: 8.

Page rationale: Identifying coping strategies, ahead of time boosts resilience. Having coping strategies at the ready can help make a good choice in moments of overwhelm. However, 'one size doesn't fit all,' everyone is unique and finds different things helpful. This page offers a variety of options that span a diverse range of coping strategies, engagement is increased by asking the child/ren to rank each one in terms of helpfulness.

Page visual:

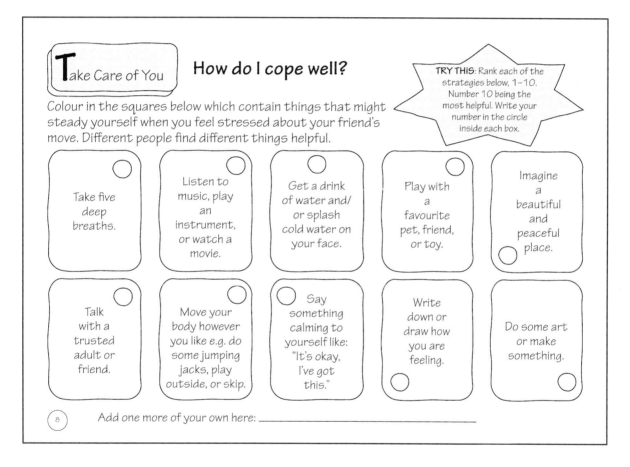

Materials needed: Each child needs: pen, pencil, rubber, sharpener, coloured pens/pencils, activity book.

Setting the scene: You may say, '*An important part of taking care of you is having coping strategies ready for when big feelings arrive. Coping strategies are things you do that lift your mood and boost wellbeing. Everyone is unique (which means special) and will have different ways of coping that work best for them.*'

Completing the activity:

1) Bring the child/ren's attention to the ten boxes on this page. Choose the most appropriate way for them to read or be lead through each of the boxes. For each box you may ask, *'Have you (or Who has) tried this and found it helpful?'* You may also like to ask, *'Have you (or Who has) not tried this, but thinks it might help?'*

Facilitator's top tip: Feel free to briefly try out some of the strategies as you move through them, for example, take a few breaths together, or do some jumping jacks.

2) Read the grey star together. Ask the child/ren to rank each of the strategies 1–10 with number 10 being the most helpful and add the number they chose inside the circle in each box.
3) Now, invite the child/ren to colour in their top three boxes to highlight the best coping strategies for them.
4) Find a way for them to share their top three. They can share this with you, their partner or you may invite popcorn responses; the children speak out their answers to the group in random order.
5) Ask them to write another coping strategy on the line provided at the bottom of the page if they have one.

Closure: You may say, *'Thank you for thinking about your favourite ways of coping. Do try some of these out, see if it's possible to notice when big feelings arrive and choose one of your ways of coping to steady yourself. Pay attention to times when you manage to do this and it helps you feel better. When this happens, congratulate yourself for taking good care of you. If you are feeling stressed, try coming back to this page to look for ideas of how to cope.'*

Extension activity: You might like to use a movement break to expand on the 'move your body however you like' box. Lead the child/ren with a body pat down – gently using both hands to pat different parts of their body with their hands, starting with the head, moving down to the feet and all the way up again. Encourage them to do this with kindness and gentleness.

***

Page title: Saying encouraging things to myself.

Page no: 9.

Page rationale: Cognitive behavioural psychology teaches that our 'inner critic' gets more active at times of change. Being aware of thoughts helps us resist getting swept away by them. Our internal dialogue impacts how we feel and act. This page mobilises the child's 'inner coach' – shifting the internal narrative to encouraging statements. The child is invited to ask a supportive adult and their friend who is leaving to contribute, making the page interactive and meaningful.

Page visual:

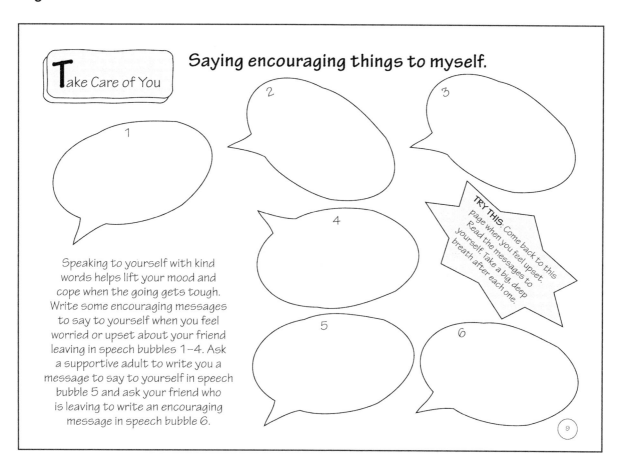

Materials needed: Each child needs: pen, pencil, rubber, sharpener, coloured pens/pencils, activity book. Optional: post it notes for child/ren to take away for extension task.

Setting the scene: You may say, '*How you speak to yourself impacts how you feel and what you do. You can choose to say kind, encouraging things that help you feel better when you* *are worried, upset or need to find courage. This page helps you think about what you can say to yourself in times of need and asks a couple of other important people to help with his too.'*

Completing the activity:

1) You may say, *'You have thoughts coming and going all the time. At times of change, like now, you'll get even more. Sometimes you'll be aware of them, sometimes not. Sometimes the thoughts are unkind, these sorts of thoughts don't make you feel good. I'm going to ask you to think of some kind messages you can tell yourself to cope well when things are tough.'*

2) You may say, *'Take your time to write down four encouraging, kind messages you'd like to hear when you need a bit of extra encouragement. Add one to each speech bubble numbered 1–4.'*

3) Give the child/ren time to write their messages down.

Facilitator's top tip: If the child/ren find it difficult to think of statements ask them to think of a helpful person in their life. Ask them what that person would say to encourage them to cope when things are tough.

4) You may like to invite sharing of one or more of their four messages. If you are working with one child, you may like to get them to read one or more of their messages aloud to you. In a group setting, you may like to get the children moving around the room sharing their messages of encouragement with each other.

Closure: You may say, *'The more you say these messages to yourself the easier they will be to recall at times of challenge – in your own time, practice saying them to yourself, always take a big, deep breath after each one. Thank you for thinking about how you speak to yourself, this is an important piece not only for 'staying well' but for life in general. If you are up for an added challenge, I'm going to ask you to add to this page by filling in speech bubbles 5 and 6. You'll need a bit of help with that. Speech bubble 5 is for a supportive adult to write you an encouraging message* (check that the child/ren have someone in mind) *and number 6 is for your friend that is leaving to do the same.'*

Facilitator's top tip: You'll need to decide how the child/ren will fill in the speech bubbles, if they are not taking their books home, find a way for them to bring the messages next time you meet them or another way to facilitate the messages being added to their page.

Facilitator's top tip: Give examples of who might be supportive adults appropriate to your setting if the child/ren can't think of anyone.

Extension Activity: You might like to invite the child/ren to write their messages on post-it notes and put them up somewhere helpful for them. Another suggestion may be to write one or more messages on their bathroom or bedroom mirror with a glass marker, so they will see the message/s daily.

***

Page title: Rainbow breathing.

Page no: 10.

Page rationale: Rainbow Breathing is a way to regulate the breath. Regulated breathing helps the mind and body to settle by triggering the bodies physiological relaxation response. Rainbow Breathing is a handy strategy for the child/ren to include in their self-regulation toolbox. The grey box, bottom right on the page, highlights the key to being able to self-regulate is to practise strategies at times when you feel okay, this trains the brain to be ready in times of need.

Page visual:

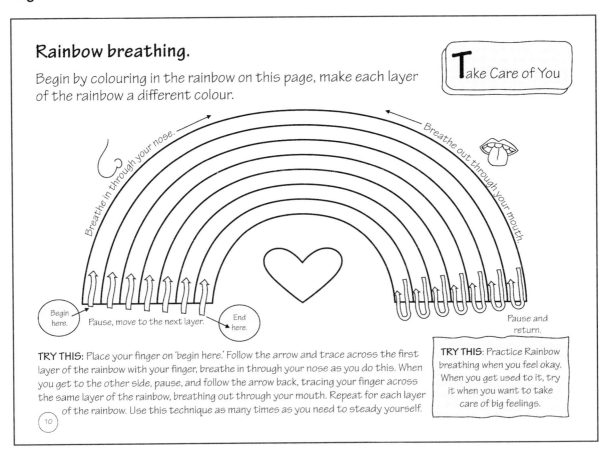

Materials needed: Each child needs: pen, pencil, rubber, sharpener, coloured pens/pencils, activity book.

Setting the scene: You may say, *'We are going to learn a breathing technique you can try when you feel stress in your body. Technique means a special way of doing something you can practise. It's called Rainbow Breathing, it will help you slow down your breathing, think more clearly and make good decisions.'*

Completing the activity:

1) Before the child/ren begin you may ask them to choose one word to describe how their mind and body feels – give an example of your own, *e.g. 'My mind feels busy, my body feels heavy'* There is no right or wrong. Challenge the child/ren to stick to one word. Invite sharing.

2) Ask the child/ren to colour in their rainbow, making each layer a different colour. They may also decorate the heart in the centre, if they choose.

3) Guide them through the instructions for Rainbow Breathing where it says TRY THIS: on the page.

4) When you have led them through Rainbow Breathing, repeat step 1), above. You might like to reflect on their answer(s) by highlighting (if appropriate), *'Rainbow Breathing has helped your body and mind relax.'*

Facilitator's top tip: You may choose to begin your next session with Rainbow Breathing creating a link between one session and the next.

Closure: Bring the child/ren's attention to the grey box at the bottom-right of the page, encourage them to practise their Rainbow Breathing when they feel okay, to be able to use it when big feelings arrive. You may give them a challenge to practice Rainbow Breathing every day for the next few days.

Extension Activity: To help the child/ren stay connected to Rainbow Breathing, you might encourage them to teach this skill to someone else and to report back next time you meet.

You may like to copy and share this pocket-sized card to help them practise.

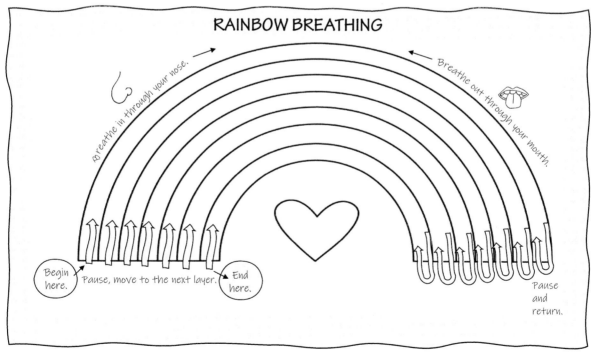

RAINBOW BREATHING

Breathe in through your nose.

Breathe out through your mouth.

Begin here.   Pause, move to the next layer.   End here.

Pause and return.

***

23

Page title: Taking my pencil for a walk.

Page no: 11.

Page rationale: This page asks 'the stayer' to mindfully create a design to colour. Many children (and adults) use mindful colouring a way to anchor themselves in the present moment. Used as a regulation strategy, a creative exercise such as this, is a way to remind our body and mind how to relax. The more often we engage in relaxing activities the better we get at being mindful. This page is credited to Peter O'Brien, a wise and talented educator who shares this activity with the children in his care.

Page visual:

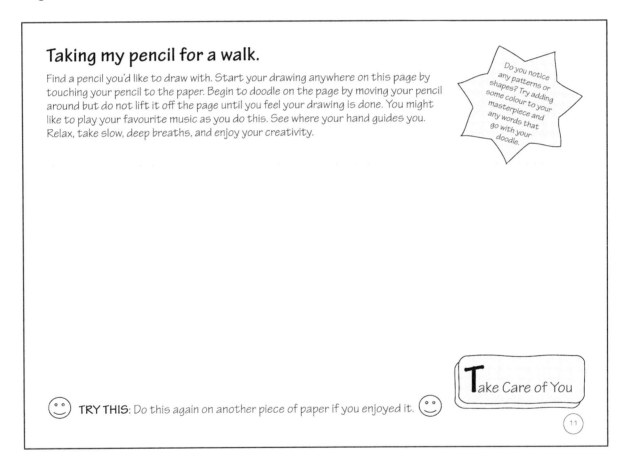

Materials needed: Each child needs: pen, pencil, rubber, sharpener, coloured pens/pencils, activity book. Optional: music, timer, a variety of different pencils and pens.

Setting the scene: You may say, *'This page is called taking my pencil for a walk. It's a mindful drawing and colouring activity. When you are mindful you choose where to place your attention. For this exercise you will place your attention on drawing and colouring.*

When you choose to focus on something in this way, your mind rests in the present, rather than worrying about what's going to happen or has happened. Being mindful helps your body relax too.'

Facilitator's top tip: The child/ren may ask you, 'What is the present?' You may say, *'The present is right now, not in the past or the future. For example, can you notice three green things you can see now?'* Get them to do this briefly. You may say, *'When you do this, you are placing your attention on what you can see in the present.'*

Completing the activity:

1) Before the child/ren begin, you may to ask them to choose one word to describe how their mind and body feels– give an example of your own, *e.g. 'My mind feels busy, my body feels heavy'* There is no right or wrong. Challenge the child/ren to stick to one word. Invite sharing.

Facilitator's top tip: You might like to show the class/child an example of a completed page to see how their page may look. Or demonstrate the activity before the child/ren begin.

2) You may say, *'Start this exercise by finding a pencil that you'd like to draw with. Can you do this now? Show me you are ready by holding you pencil high up in the air.'*
3) You may say, *'Now, touch the page with your pencil and begin to move it around but do not lift it off the page until your drawing feels complete. It's just like taking your pencil for a walk around your page. You can make big or small movements, straight lines, wiggly lines, shapes. There's no right or wrong. Remember, don't take your pencil off the page until you are done.'*

Facilitator's top tip: Consider playing some relaxing music as they draw on their page.

4) Once they have begun drawing you may say: *'As you move your pencil around, notice your feet flat on the floor, give your feet a little wiggle if you like.'*
5) Once the child/ren have lifted their pencil off the page. Invite them to sit back in their chair, notice their feet on the floor again and their body in contact with the chair. Ask them to look at their page and see if they notice any patterns or shapes.
6) Ask them to add any words to their page, if they wish.
7) Invite them to begin colouring in their page.

Facilitator's top tip: Have a variety of different pens and pencils accessible, so that the child/ren stay seated whilst colouring.

8) As they are colouring you may say, *'As you colour, notice your breathing, be aware you are breathing in and out. You might like to make the in breath and the out breath slightly longer.'*

Facilitator's top tip: Children will progress with this page at different rates, you might like to set a timer.

9) At the end of this exercise, repeat step 1) from the start of this activity. You might like to reflect on their answer(s) by highlighting (if appropriate); *'Isn't it curious how drawing and colouring has made a difference to your body and mind?'*

Closure: You may say: *'Every time you practice being creative like this you are reminding your body and mind how to relax. You might like to try this activity on another piece of paper another time. It may help when you notice stress showing up in your body to steady yourself. It was great to see you taking care of you by being creative today.'*

Extension Activity: You might like to ask the artist/s to give their piece a title. If you are working with one child, you might like to set up a role play; invite the child to pretend their artwork is in an exhibition. Tell them you are a visitor to the exhibition and challenge them, as the artist, to tell you the title and as much as they can about their piece.

In a group setting you may invite group members to introduce (using the art exhibition example above, if you wish) their artwork one by one, sharing the title and something brief about their creation.

Perhaps creating an interactive gallery of sorts appeals; you may like to get the children moving around the room, sharing their piece with another child, then moving to another when they are ready, or on your signal.

Another suggestion is to create a gallery by laying out the artworks for the group to view.

***

Page title: My circle of support.

Page no: 12.

Page rationale: This page helps 'the stayer' acknowledge and name people from different spheres of their life who can help them get through this time of change. This increases the chances of the child choosing to connect with key helpers in times of need. This activity is grounding and helps the child feel safe and supported.

Page visual:

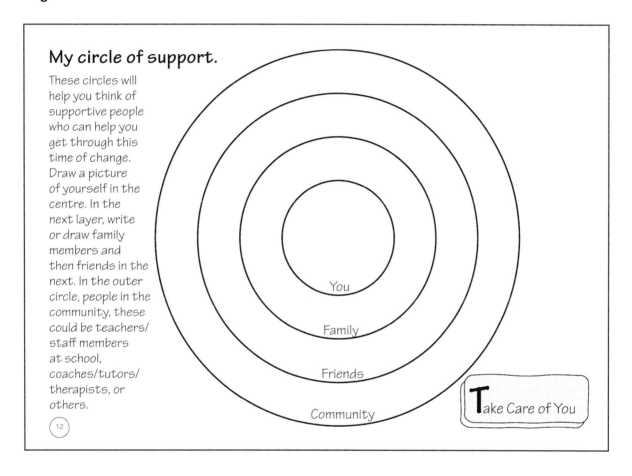

My circle of support.

These circles will help you think of supportive people who can help you get through this time of change. Draw a picture of yourself in the centre. In the next layer, write or draw family members and then friends in the next. In the outer circle, people in the community, these could be teachers/ staff members at school, coaches/tutors/ therapists, or others.

12

You

Family

Friends

Community

Take Care of You

Materials needed: Each child needs: pen, pencil, rubber, sharpener, coloured pens/pencils, activity book. Optional: timer, downloaded templates for people paper chain, glue, scissors and a way to print images.

Setting the scene: You may say, '*The circles on this page will help you think of who can help you at this time of change. It will remind you of supportive people you have around you whom you can ask for help.*'

Completing the activity:

1) You may say, *'You are in the centre of your circle of support. The first thing to do is to draw a picture of yourself in the centre, inside the circle that says "You." This can be a self-portrait, colours, shapes, lines, or squiggles to represent you.'*

Facilitator's top tip: Have a variety of different pens and pencils accessible, so the child/ren stay seated whilst colouring. You may also consider supporting the child/ren to print a photo of themsleves to stick in the centre, if time, and resources allow.

Facilitator's top tip: Children will progress with this page at different rates, you might like to set a timer.

2) Invite the child/ren to move to the next layer and add supportive family members. They can draw them, write their names and/or draw a symbol to represent them.
3) Repeat step 2), above for the friends circle.
4) For the outer circle, you may say, *'Now it's time for the outer circle, this one is for supportive people in your community, these people could be teachers, staff members at school, coaches, tutors, therapists or others'* (make these examples fit your setting and the children you are working with). Again, they can draw them, write their names and/or draw a symbol to represent them.

Closure: You may say, *'Well done, your circle of support is now complete. Lean back in your chair, look carefully at your page, and take a moment to notice what it feels like to see all these people who can help you get through this time of change. Remember everyone asks for help sometimes. It's likely you are going to need more support than usual in this time of your friend leaving.'* If time permits, you might ask the child/ren to name the feeling that is evoked by looking at their page.

Extension Activity: Follow the instructions below which invites the child/ren to bring their supporters to life by making a people paper chain.

People Paper Chain: Creating a people paper chain could be done with you facilitating or the child/ren may complete this in their own time.

1) Print the paper people chain on the next page, enlarge as desired:

2) Guide the children through steps i–iv) below.

Facilitator's top tip: You may choose to demonstrate the process with your own paper people sheet. You may also like to show the child/ren an example of a finished chain.

    i) Cut along all dotted lines so that you have two rectangles and two paper people templates. If you are supporting one for the child, one for you and one for them. In a group setting, one page will give two children paper people templates.

    ii) Take one of the templates and fold all the solid lines, into four sections, making sure the person outline can be seen on the top.

    iii) Carefully cut out the person outline, cutting through all the layers of folded paper. BE SURE TO LEAVE THE HANDS INTACT!

    iv) Carefully unfold to see your paper people chain.

3) Encourage the child/ren to choose four supportive people they identified in their 'Circle of support' exercise. Each of their paper chain people represents one of these four.

4) Invite them to get creative by decorating their four people and encourage them to put them up somewhere they will see them often to remind them of who to ask for help.

***

Page title: The magic of Vitamin N (N = NATURE).

Page no: 13.

Page rationale: M. Amos Clifford, founder of the Association of Nature and Forest Therapy Guides and Programs, advocates that spending time in nature boosts wellbeing. This page raises awareness that this can take a variety of forms. The visualisation on this page helps to connect with a special place in nature, real or imagined. This activity promotes a regulatory effect. The integration task in the bottom-right box helps to cement this activity.

Page visual:

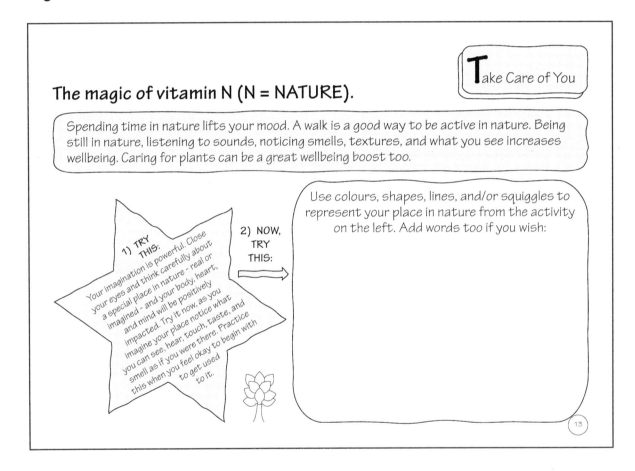

Materials needed: Each child needs: pen, pencil, rubber, sharpener, coloured pens/pencils, activity book.

Setting the scene: You may say, '*This page is about soaking up some Vitamin N – as you can see on your page N=Nature. Spending time in nature lifts your mood, going for a cycle* *or walk is one way to do this. Pausing in nature, by being still and tuning into your senses can also boost wellbeing.'* Ask the children if they can name their five senses. Go through each and relate these to being in nature, highlight to take caution with taste and touch in the wild. Let them know that caring for plants can give a wellbeing boost too.

Completing the activity:

1) Ask the child/ren what they already do in nature that lifts their mood. Gather examples.
2) You may say, *'We are going to try an activity now that uses your powerful imagination. Your mind, heart and body can get a wellbeing boost even by thinking carefully about a special place in nature. This might be a real place you know, or an imaginary place.'*
3) Lead the child/ren through the 'Special place in nature visualisation' script, below. It is designed to lead the child/ren whilst they are seated on a chair. Feel free to adjust the script if child/ren are in a different position.

Special place in nature visualisation:

'Get yourself comfortable in your seat, adjust your body position a little if you need to.

Begin by closing your eyes.

As you sit here, notice your feet in contact with the floor.

Be aware of your body sitting in the chair, notice which bits of your body are in contact with the chair, notice which parts of your body are not.

Be aware of the air around you, notice if it's warm or cold, moving or still.

Now, notice your breathing, no need to change your breathing, notice the inbreath and the outbreath. Breathing in and breathing out. Notice how your body rises on the inbreath and falls on the outbreath. (Pause).

Now, bring to mind a special place in nature. A place where you feel safe and peaceful. This could be a place you know well, it could be a place you have seen in a photograph, or an imaginary place.

Allow the image of this place to become clearer in your mind. (Pause).

Imagine you are in this special place. I am going to invite you now, to explore this special place using your senses:

Firstly, notice what you can see in this special place in nature, take in as much detail as you can, notice colours, lines, shapes, objects, there may be people, animals, buildings, trees, or water. Take a moment to look down at your clothes and shoes, notice what you are wearing. (Pause).

Notice what you can see close to, and far away in your peaceful place. (Pause).

Next, using your sense of hearing, notice what can be heard in your special place, it could be the natural sounds of animals, the weather, the ocean, the forest, people. Tune into the sounds you can hear. (Pause).

Now, using your sense of touch. Notice what is here to be felt in your special place in nature. Feel whatever you are sitting on, or if you are standing or lying down sensing into what it feels like to be in contact with whatever is underneath you. You may be able to feel the touch of your clothes on your skin or the air around you. You may like to move around your special place in nature now or reach out to touch objects that call for your attention. (Pause).

Moving to the sense of smell, now. Take a long, deep breath, breathe in the energy this place gives you and breathe out again. On the next deep inbreath notice what is in your special place to be smelled. (Pause).

Lastly, tune into your sense of taste. What can you taste while you are here, in your special place in nature? It might be something that you are eating or have eaten in this place. It might be a favourite taste. (Pause).

You might like to spend a little longer connecting with this place, noticing whatever calls for your attention. (Pause).

Letting your special place in nature go now. Knowing that you can come back here anytime you need to.

Becoming aware of your breathing again, your inbreath and outbreath. Breathing in and breathing out, your body rising and falling. (Pause).

Becoming aware again of your body sitting in the chair, the parts in contact with the chair and those not.

Notice your feet in contact with the floor.

Now, open your eyes, come back into this room.'

4) To encourage reflection; you may ask *'What did you discover during the activity?'* Invite discussion, either with you, in pairs or whole group sharing.

5) Invite the children to use colours shapes, lines and/or squiggles to represent their special place in nature in the box, bottom-right on their page. They may also add any words that fit with their place that they visited in the visualisation too.

Closure: You may say, *'Thank you for thinking about the magic of Vitamin N. I hope this page has inspired you to think of ways to enjoy nature, real or imagined. I'd like to give you a challenge to choose to go outside and spend time in nature before we meet again and see how it boosts your wellbeing. Have a go at tuning into your five senses when you are there. Remember, your imagination is powerful, and you can practice the visualisation we tried today to lift your mood.'*

Extension activity: You may like to try the activity below.

Stand like a tree exercise:

1) You may say, *"We are going to try an activity called "Stand like a tree." This shows you a way to be mindful, when you are mindful you choose where to place your attention in the present moment. You are going to pretend to be a tree. Even in windy weather trees are strong, solid, firmly rooted to the ground. This is a great exercise to try when you need to feel strong and brave."*

Facilitator's top tip: The child/ren may ask you, 'What is the present moment?' You may say, *'The present moment is right now, not in the past or the future. For example, can you pay attention to what you can hear now?'* Get them to do this briefly. You may say, *'When you do this, you are placing your attention on sounds that are happening in this present moment.'*

2) Ensure the child/ren have enough space so they won't hit any objects or other children around them. Get them to practice swinging their arms to make sure they are in a good spot before you begin.

3) Lead the activity, slowly, moving through these steps:

   i) Stand still, notice your feet firmly planted on the ground.
   ii) Stand tall, extend your neck and head upwards, lift your chin slightly.
   iii) Drop your shoulders back and down.
   iv) Imagine that a gentle breeze is making your body sway, and your arms gently move, keep your feet firmly planted. Gently let your body sway.
   v) Imagine the wind getting stronger, make your body movements bigger, keep your feet rooted.
   vi) Imagine the weather has passed. Stand still, notice how that feels.
   vii) Take a few deep breaths and say to yourself 'I am like a tree, brave and strong whatever the weather.'

4) Ask the child/ren what they can learn from this exercise? You might say, *"At the end of the exercise I asked you to say to yourself 'I am like a tree, brave and strong whatever the weather.' What does it teach us about change?"* Hopefully they will share, difficult times don't last forever, challenges come and go like the weather. They may say that even though, I feel stressed sometimes I can cope by staying steady, strong, and grounded. If they are not forthcoming you might say, *'We might think of this time of change as a bit like the weather, it will not last forever, if you can stay strong and steady like a tree you can get through it, as best you can.'*

Facilitator's top tip: If time and location allow, you may do this exercise outside in a natural setting.

5) Encourage the child/ren to practice this exercise in their own time. You may say, *'It's important to practise standing like a tree when you feel okay. When you get used it try it at a time you need to be brave and strong.'*

***

Page title: Creative connections.

Page no: 14.

Page rationale: This page covers the letter R-section of the TRUST acronym, 'Remain in contact.' Planning how the child will stay connected with their friends may boost the longevity of their friendship and increase the chances of them staying in touch.

Page visual:

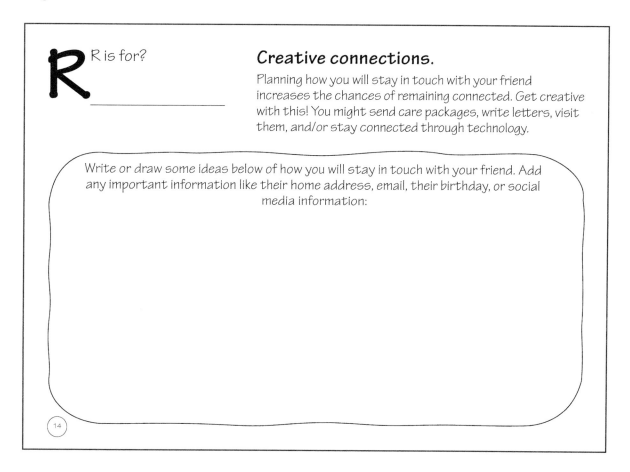

Materials needed: Each child needs: pen, pencil, rubber, sharpener, coloured pens/pencils, activity book.

Setting the scene: You may say, '*This is a page for you to plan how you will stay in contact with your friend. There are lots of different ways you can do this. This page will help you make sure you have important information to hand after their departure. This makes it easier to remain in contact.*'

Completing the activity:

1) Begin by inviting the child/ren to fill in the **R is for** _____ on their page. You may say, *'We arrive at the second letter of* TRUST. *Can you remember what R stands for? (Elicit from the child/ren: Remain in contact')*

2) You may say, *'Let's brainstorm some ideas of how you can remain in contact with your friend.'*

3) In a group setting, invite the children to 'popcorn' – call out in random order some ideas. Find a way to record ideas for the group and ask them to write or draw suggestions they like on their page. If you are supporting one child you can do this in a more discursive manner, encourage recording of ideas on their page as they go.

4) Ask the child/ren to record specific contact information, the date of their friend's birthday if they know it. If not, ask them to add this information when they have found it out.

Closure: You may say, *'Thanks for getting all your ideas and information down. If there are things that you didn't know, feel free to add these later, perhaps next time we look at this book together again.* (Teachers/therapists - if the books are going home, they can add these details before they return).'

***

Page title: What my body tells me.

Page no: 15.

Page rationale: This page begins the letter U-section of the TRUST acronym, 'Unload feelings.' The child is encouraged to acknowledge a variety of feelings and how they show up in their body. Being able to name and share feelings has a regulatory effect. Dan Siegel, Professor of Psychiatry at UCLA School of Medicine coined the concept 'name it to tame it.' Naming feelings reduces their intensity, which helps to gain a greater sense of control. This page helps the child/ren name a number of feelings and to understand it's normal to experience a range of feelings at times of change, and all are okay. 'The stayer' is invited to consider their somatic experience of a range of emotions by annotating the body outline, this develops interoception. Interoception is the ability to sense signals from the body, when interoception is honed our ability to answer the question 'how do I feel?' at any given moment is increased. Kelly Mahler, a world-renowned Occupational Therapist, says that interoception has a huge influence on many areas of our lives like self-regulation, mental health, and social connection.

Page visual:

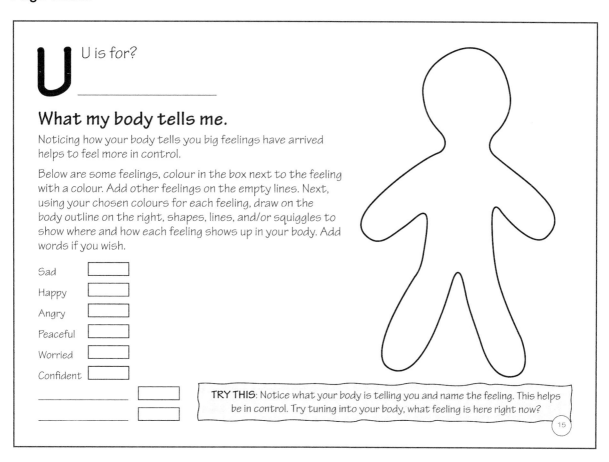

U is for?
_____

What my body tells me.
Noticing how your body tells you big feelings have arrived helps to feel more in control.

Below are some feelings, colour in the box next to the feeling with a colour. Add other feelings on the empty lines. Next, using your chosen colours for each feeling, draw on the body outline on the right, shapes, lines, and/or squiggles to show where and how each feeling shows up in your body. Add words if you wish.

Sad ☐
Happy ☐
Angry ☐
Peaceful ☐
Worried ☐
Confident ☐
_____ ☐
_____ ☐

TRY THIS: Notice what your body is telling you and name the feeling. This helps be in control. Try tuning into your body, what feeling is here right now?

15

Materials needed: Each child needs: pen, pencil, rubber, sharpener, coloured pens/pencils, activity book.

Setting the scene: You may say, *'Your body will tell you when big feelings arrive. Feelings are like visitors, they don't stay for long but while they are here, they have something to teach us about ourselves. This page will help us notice where we feel big feelings in our body. Once we get better at this we can be more in control.'*

Completing the activity:

1) Begin by inviting the child/ren to fill in the **U is for** _____ on their page. You may say, *'We arrive at our third letter of* TRUST. *Can you remember what U stands for? (Elicit from the child/ren: Unload feelings.')*

2) *You may say, 'Have a look at the feelings written on your page. They are sad, happy, angry, peaceful, worried, and confident.'* These feelings are not good or bad, they are like signposts that provide important information. Noticing and and naming feelings helps to understand ourselves better.'

3) Next, invite the child/ren to fill in the box next to the feeling with a different colour for each.

4) Using their chosen colour for each feeling invite the child/ren to draw shapes, lines and/or squiggles to show where and how each feeling shows up in their body inside the body outline on their page.

5) Ask the child/ren to add any words to their body outline that fit too.

6) Encourage the child/ren to add another feeling, or two to the blank spaces, bottom-left of the page, invite them to repeat steps 3–5) above.

Facilitator's top tip: You may choose to have a list of feelings words for the child/ren to use for step 6) above.

7) If time permits, you may like to ask the child/ren to share which feelings they have at this time of their friend leaving. In this discussion re-enforce where they feel the emotion(s) in their body.

Closure: You may say, *'Aren't our bodies clever? They let you know when big feelings arise so you can be 'the boss' of your feelings. This page teaches you to pay careful attention to your body and notice when it lets you know that big feelings have arrived. Naming the feeling and being curious to how it is showing up in your body can be powerful. The next page goes into this idea deeper, are you ready to do some experimenting?'*

***

Page title: Draw feelings out.

Page no: 16.

Page rationale: Acknowledging and accepting feelings helps to cope better when tricky emotions arrive. Dr. Peter Levine, founder of Somatic Experiencing, highlights that becoming curious about body sensations and their qualities is healing. This page follows Levine's wisdom and invites the child/ren to engage with the qualities of a chosen feeling. It encourages a playful and curious approach for navigating the emotional landscape.

Page visual:

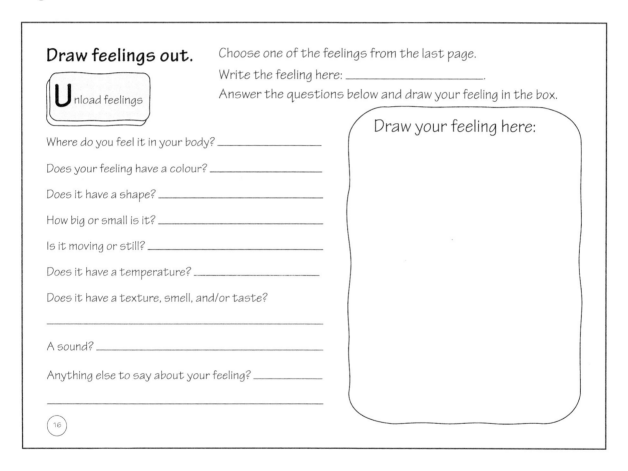

Materials needed: Each child needs: pen, pencil, rubber, sharpener, coloured pens/pencils, activity book.

Setting the scene: You may say, *'Noticing feelings, naming them and being curious about them helps us take good care of emotions and feel more in control. This page invites you to be curious about a particular feeling.'*

Facilitator's top tip: The child/ren may ask you what emotion means. You may say, *'Emotion is another word for feeling.'*

Completing the activity:

1) You may say, *'Let's begin. Choose a feeling you'd like to explore. Turn back to page 15 if you need help thinking of a feeling. When you have chosen a feeling write it on the line at the top of this page.'*

Facilitator's top tip: You may have an additional resource available like a feelings wheel or list.

2) There are a variety of options for ways to answer the questions on this page. You may guide the child/ren through each question and invite them to write their answers on their page. In a group setting, the child/ren may complete this in pairs, interviewing each other, writing their partners answers for them in their book. Alternatively, you may offer a visualisation exercise with the child/ren recording their answers afterwards. If you choose the latter, you might like to follow the script for 'Exploring a feeling visualisation,' below (if you chose NOT to do this exercise go to step 3).

Exploring a feeling visualisation: The script below is designed to lead the child/ren whilst seated on a chair. Feel free to adjust the script if the child/ren are in a different position.

Facilitator's top tip: Some children will silently notice answers during this activity. Some may answer you aloud. There is no right or wrong way to do this.

'Get yourself comfortable in your seat, adjust your body position a little if you need to.

Begin by closing your eyes if that feels comfortable for you.

As you sit here, notice your feet in contact with the floor. Be aware of your body sitting in the chair, notice which bits of your body are in contact with the chair, notice which parts of your body are not.

Be aware of the air around you, notice if it's warm or cold, moving or still. Notice your breathing, no need to change your breathing, notice the inbreath and the outbreath.

Breathing in and breathing out. Notice how your body rises on the inbreath and falls on the outbreath.

Now, bring to mind the feeling that you'd like to get curious about. Name the feeling silently to yourself. Whilst you keep your eyes closed, I'm going to ask you questions. Notice the answers that come, there is no right or wrong.

Where do you feel your feeling when it arises, in your body? (Pause).

If your feeling had a colour, what would it be? It may be one colour, more than one colour. Notice the shade of the colour is it bright, dark, or light? (Pause).

Perhaps your feeling has a shape? It could be a recognisable shape or something new. (Pause).

Notice how big your feeling is; is it big, medium, or small? (Pause).

Is your feeling moving or still? If it's moving, it might be fast or slow. (Pause).

Imagine you could reach out and touch your feeling. Would it be hot, cold, or warm? As you reach out and touch your feeling, notice if it has a texture, it could be bumpy or smooth, soft, hard or furry. (Pause).

As you sit with this feeling, take a deep breath in and out. Does your feeling have a smell?

It might even have a taste, notice what this might be, it could be a new taste or a favourite taste. (Pause).

Is there a sound that goes along with your feeling? (Pause).

Take another deep breath in and out. Do you notice anything else about your feeling? (Pause).

Let your feeling go now. Knowing you can come back and connect with it anytime you need to.

Becoming aware of your breathing again, your inbreath and outbreath. Breathing in and breathing out, your body rising and falling. (Pause).

Becoming aware, again, of your body sitting here in the chair, the parts in contact with the chair and those not.

Notice your feet in contact with the floor.

Now gently open your eyes, come back into this room.'

Facilitator's top tip: If time allows, you might like to ask the child/ren what they discovered during the exercise and invite them to share verbally.

3) Ask the child/ren to fill in the left-hand side of their page with the answers to the questions.

4) Invite the child/ren to draw their feeling in the box on the right-hand side of the page. Let them know that it can look like something or be more abstract using, colours, shapes, lines, and/or squiggles.

5) Invite the child/ren to share their page and say as little or as much as they would like about it; they can do this with you or each other in a group setting.

Closure: You may say, *'Thanks for using your curiosity today. It's been interesting hearing about your feelings. Remember, getting to know feelings can help you feel more in control, which is especially helpful at times of change.'*

Extension activity: If time allows, invite the child/ren to share one thing they'd like to remember after completing this page.

***

Page title: Feelings focus.

Page no: 17.

Page rationale: There are many ways you can express how you feel. The more creative you get the better. Everyone is unique and will prefer different ways to express. This page offers a variety of options for unloading feelings and helps the child/ren to acknowledge their preferred ways of taking good care of their feelings. It makes a link between their somatic experience and choosing a way to express their emotions. The invitation to tick off the strategies increases the chances of the child giving a range of techniques a go.

Page visual:

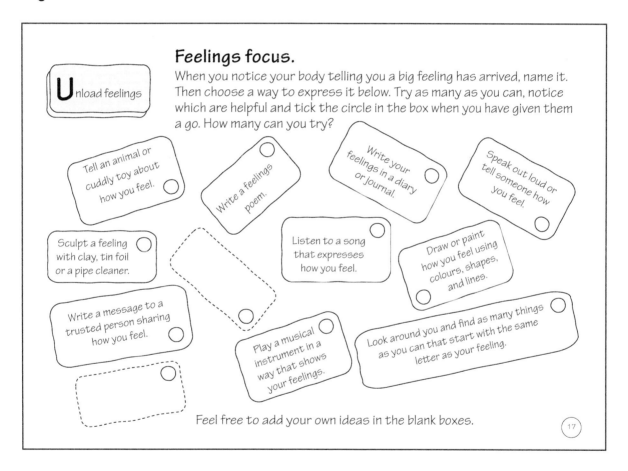

Materials needed: Each child needs: pen, pencil, rubber, sharpener, coloured pens/pencils, activity book.

Setting the scene: You may say, *'This page helps you think of creative ways to unload feelings. The page encourages you to name your feeling and choose a way to express it.*

Remember, we are all unique and what we find helpful differs from person to person. It's good to know what your preferred ways of taking care of your feelings are, so you can be ready when big feelings arrive'.

Completing the activity:

1) You may say: *'Have a look at the boxes on this page, they offer some ideas of how to take good care of your feelings. Take some time to read through them now.'* Or you may like to read them aloud yourself to the child/ren.
2) Invite the child/ren to colour in boxes they find helpful or might find helpful.
3) Invite the child/ren to add another strategy or two in the blank boxes on the page, something they already do or a new idea they would like to try.
4) Bring the child/ren's attention to the box that says, 'Look around you and find as many things as you can that start with the same letter as your feeling.'
5) Invite each child to name a feeling they have right now. Once they have done this, ask them where they feel this in their body.
6) Next, ask them to take the first letter of their feeling and either silently or out loud notice five things in the room that begin with the same letter. When they have completed this, they can place a tick in the small circle within the bottom-right box on their page.

Closure: You may say, *'There are so many ways you can unload feelings, do pay attention to times when you manage to use one of these strategies and it helps you feel better. When this happens, congratulate yourself for taking good care of your feelings and tick off that strategy in the small circle inside the box. If you are feeling stressed, try coming back to this page to look for ideas of how to help yourself.'*

***

Page title: Gratitude banner.

Page no: 18.

Page rationale: Gratitude is the act of recognising and acknowledging good things that happen, resulting in a state of appreciation. Martin Seligman, world-renowned psychologist, states that expressing gratitude can positively impact wellbeing. This page introduces gratitude, inviting an intentional practice of noticing things to be grateful for. The hope is that this awakens gratitude within the child, helping them 'stay well.'

Page visual:

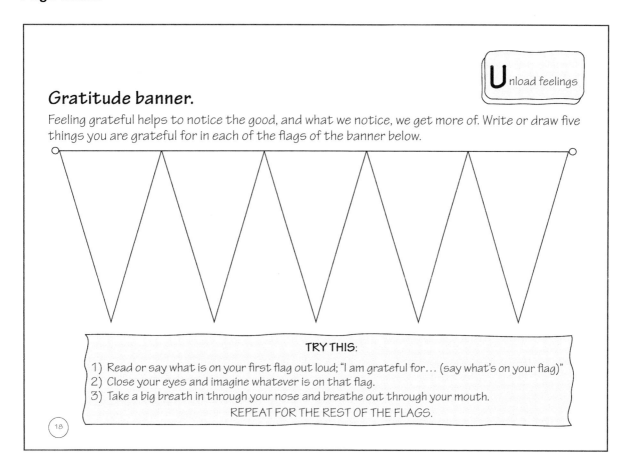

Materials needed: Each child needs: pen, pencil, rubber, sharpener, coloured pens/pencils, activity book. Optional: timer.

Setting the scene: You may say, *'Today we are going to practice being grateful. Being grateful is when you feel thankful for the good things in your life, like friends, food, water,* *your home. Gratitude is about taking a moment to reflect on things you appreciate, big or small. Doing this gives you a wellbeing boost.'*

Completing the activity:

1) You may say, *'Let's begin by thinking of a few things you are grateful for. These can be big things like your family, or school or they can be everyday things like drinking a nice glass or water or cuddling your pet.'* If you are supporting one child brainstorm some ideas (do share examples of your own too). If you are in a group setting, find a way to gather ideas from the group.

Facilitator's top tip: You may consider setting a timer for one minute and inviting the child/ren to write down as many things they are thankful for as they can. Invite sharing afterwards.

2) Once you have some examples, ask the child/ren to begin populating their banner by writing or drawing one thing they are thankful for on each flag.

Facilitator's top tip: Highlight that each banner will be unique as everyone is different and are thankful for different things.

Facilitator's top tip: If you are in a group setting, some children may finish before others. Invite those who have completed their banner to add colour, shapes, lines and/or squiggles to their flags, making their banner unique.

3) Next, bring the child/ren's attention to the grey box at the bottom of the page. Guide them through the activity. If you are supporting a group, you may like to get them to speak the sentence in unision, 'I am grateful for (they add what ever they have on their flag.)' Get the children to close their eyes for the next part of the activity. Invite them to take a deep breath in unison. Repeat this for the remaining four flags.

Closure: You may say, *'Noticing what you feel grateful for everyday lifts mood, and helps you deal better with change.'* If you are a parent supporting your child, you may say, *'Come back to this page at a time that suits you every day for a week and do the exercise in the grey box again. I'd be so interested to hear how it's helpful.'* If you are in a school/therapy setting you may like to say the same if the child/ren take the activity books home. If not, you may say, *'You might like to continue being grateful until we meet again. If so, you might notice three things you are grateful for every night before bed or when you get up in the morning. I'd be interested to know how you get on.'*

Extension activity: You may like to try the activities below.

Gratitude Jar: You might like to create a gratitude jar that stores paper slips, each slip has written on it one thing that the person who wrote it is grateful for. If you are a parent, you could help your child create a jar and add one slip to it every day, after a few weeks you can look at all the slips together or invite the child to pull one out to connect with gratefulness from time to time. You may consider having a family Gratitude Jar. In a therapy/class setting you could create something similar. Don't forget to help the child/ren decorate the gratitude jar, you can design special slips if you choose. Find a good spot for it to be placed.

Gratitude banner: You may like to help the child/ren create a big banner that hangs up somewhere. Each flag is something to be grateful for. This can be added to over time. It may be a project for one child, a group, or the family.

***

Page title: Purposeful planning.

Page no: 19.

Page rationale: This page begins the letter S-section of the TRUST acronym, 'Say goodbye.' An important part of 'staying well' is getting goodbyes right. This involves planning and doing. Interestingly, Dr. Douglas W. Ota says that goodbyes are often avoided as they are inherently painful in nature, however, he stresses their importance for optimal departure for both the 'leaver' and 'the stayer.' This makes planning and preparation key.

Page visual:

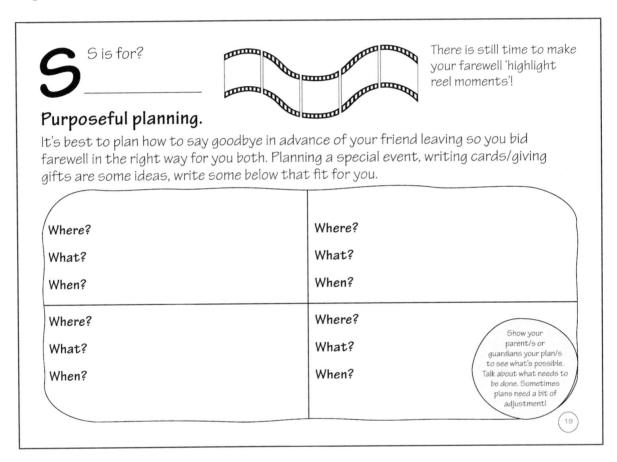

Materials needed: Each child needs: pen, pencil, rubber, sharpener, coloured pens/pencils, activity book.

Setting the scene: You may say, '*No matter which way you look at it, goodbyes are tough. Sometimes goodbyes are avoided as people think they might be painful. But, saying* *goodbye in the right way is healthy, it's a chance to celebrate your friendship, make a lasting memory and to show your friend how important they are to you.'*

1) Begin by inviting the child/ren to fill in the **S is for** _____ on their page. You may say, *'We arrive at the fourth letter of* TRUST. *Can you remember what S stands for? (Elicit from the child/ren: Say goodbye.')*

2) Highlight this page is called 'Purposeful planning.' Read the paragraph at the top of the page, or ask the child/ren to read it silently to themselves, or aloud.

3) You may say, *'We are going to think about how to say goodbye now. This is unique to you, everyone chooses a different way of doing this. It can be arranging something that costs nothing like a football match in a park, an event where you visit somewhere, a goodbye party or taking cupcakes to a last session or class. You've probably got lots of ideas of your own.'* (Ensure that suggestions fit your setting).

4) Invite the child/ren to fill in the first Where?, What?, When?, (top-left).

5) Find a way for them to share what they have written with you, a partner or the group.

6) Invite them to repeat this with one or more of the boxes on the page, if they have any other ideas. In a group setting the children may glean some ideas from each other.

7) Ask the child/ren to turn back to the beginning of their activity book, to page 1. Read the quote to the child/ren or ask them to read it themesleves. Encourage them to reflect on what it means to them. Draw out that there are lots of ways to stay in touch if they choose to.

8) Ask them to turn back to page 19. Highlight the paragraph, top-right of the page which mentions there is still time for them to make their farewells 'highlight reel moments!'

Closure: You may say, *'Plans for goodbyes will need to be discussed with your parent/s or guardian as you'll, most likely, need their help. Plans may need to be adjusted, prepare to be flexible and open to ideas. Sometimes the planning part can be almost as much fun as the actual event.'*

***

Page title: Goodbye Card for my friend.

Page no: 20.

Page rationale: This page supports the child to create a goodbye card for their friend, a gesture that lets their friend know that the friendship is appreciated and may cement continuing connection. This activity promotes closure by acceptance of forthcoming change.

Page visual:

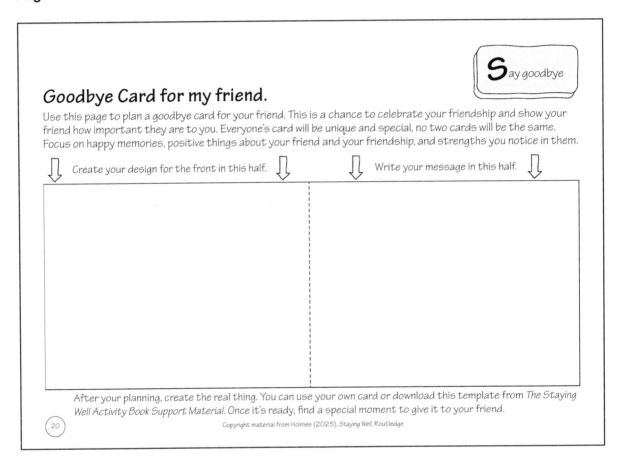

Materials needed: Each child needs: pen, pencil, rubber, sharpener, coloured pens/pencils, activity book. Optional: music, additional decorating material, card to make the final piece or the downloaded template.

Setting the scene: You may say, '*Now, you are going get creative and design a goodbye card. This is a chance to celebrate your friendship and show your friend how important they are to you. Everyone's card will be unique and special, no two cards will be the same.*'

Completing the activity:

1) You may say, '*We are going to use this page to plan what your card will look like. Use the left-hand side to create the design and the right to plan what to write inside the card. Focus on happy memories, positive things about your friend and your friendship and strengths you notice in them.*'

Facilitator's top tip: Consider having a card ready to share as an example.

2) Give the child/ren time to create their design and write the words they would like to write in their card. Support as necessary.
3) Choose when the child/ren make their actual card. It may be in your time with them or something that they do independently.

Facilitator's top tip: You may choose to provide the child/ren with some card or download the template from the *Staying Well Activity Book Support Material* for them to use for their actual card.

Facilitator's top tip: If they make their card with you, you may choose to play some relaxing music while they create.

Facilitator's top tip: You may wish to provide additional material, glitter, glue, metallic pens, things to stick onto the card or if resources allow to support the child/ren in printing of some photos/images.

Closure: You may say, '*Thank you for your creativity today, it's been wonderful to see you think carefully about what to draw and write. Once your goodbye card is ready, find a special moment to give it to your friend.*'

***

Page title: A message from my friend.

Page no: 21.

Page rationale: This page invites the child to ask their friend to create something for them, a drawing or note that may become a keepsake, a physical reminder of their important friendship. Like the previous page, this activity promotes closure by acceptance of the forthcoming change.

Page visual:

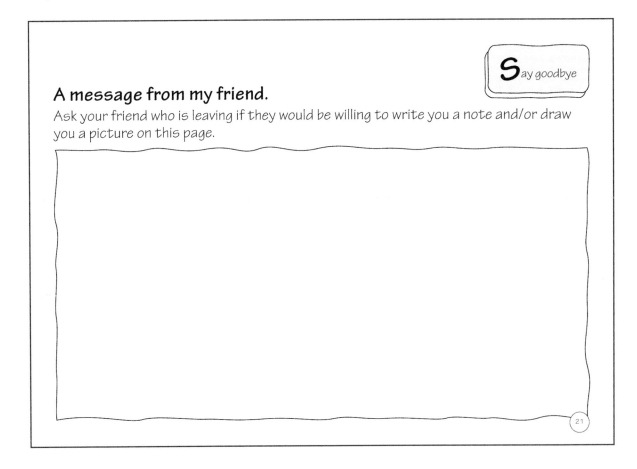

Materials needed: Each child needs: pen, pencil, rubber, sharpener, coloured pens/pencils, activity book.

Setting the scene: You may say, '*This page is for your friend to write you a message on, you can choose to pass them your* Staying Well Activity Book *or ask them to create something you can stick in.*' (Make this fit your arrangements for the activity books, in a school/therapeutic setting it will depend if the books go home with the child or not.)

Completing the activity:

1) Support the child/ren to think about the best time to ask their friend to do this.

Closure: You may say, '*When this page has your friend's message on it will become very special. You may find it helpful to read it when you need a bit of a boost to remind you how important the friendship is to you. Don't forget to remind yourself of the quote that is on the first page of this activity book: 'Goodbyes may not be forever, goodbyes may not be the end, they simply mean farewell until you meet again.'*

***

Page title: Cool connections.

Page no: 22.

Page rationale: This page begins the last section of the TRUST acronym, 'Take opportunities.' It encourages 'the stayer' to use their bravery to take opportunities to settle once their friend has gone. Awareness is raised of the importance of ongoing connections with others and the page helps the child to think of activities that might foster a wider circle of friends. There is also an acknowledgement that re-calibration after their friend has gone may take time and patience is needed.

Page visual:

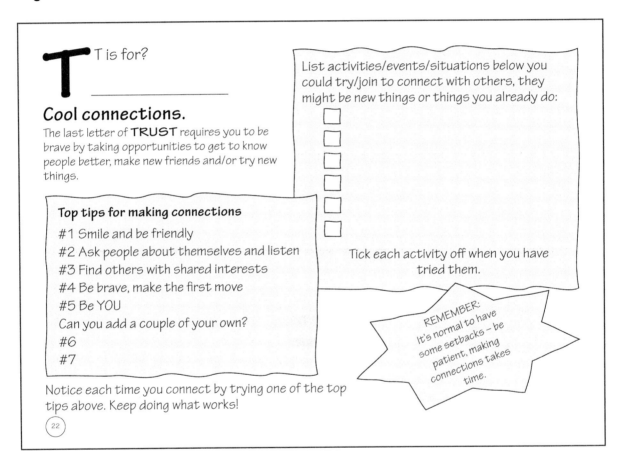

Materials needed: Each child needs: pen, pencil, rubber, sharpener, coloured pens/pencils, activity book.

Setting the scene: You may say, '*This page helps you recognise opportunities to boost connection. Your friend leaving may mean you'll need to be brave, to try to find others* *to hang out with and feel connected to. You'll think about things that make this easier and of activities that make this possible.'*

Completing the activity:

1) Begin by inviting the child/ren to fill in the **T is for** _____ on their page. You may say, *'We arrive at our second T, the last letter of letter of* TRUST. *Can you remember what this last letter T stands for? (Elicit from the child/ren: Take opportunities')*

2) You may say, *'This page is called Cool connections, let's begin by exploring some top tips. Have a look at the grey box, on the left of your page.'* Invite the child/ren to read these to themselves, aloud or read through the top tips with them.

3) After the five tips have been read, generate discussion. You might like to ask the child/ren which one seems the most important, which is the easiest/the hardest, which have they tried before?

4) Ask the child/ren what they would add to this list, encourage them to add a number six and seven if they wish. Find a way for sharing.

5) Bring the child/ren's attention to the grey box on the right. Support them in identifying activities they already do where connections could be made or activities they could try/ join to foster new connections. Invite them to add these next to the white boxes and tick them off when they have tried them.

Facilitator's top tip: The activity needn't be something organised, it might be to sit with a group in the school canteen, go to a specific area to connect at breaktime, it could be going to a local playground, for example, fit these to your context.

Closure: You may say, *'Notice each time you connect by trying one of the top tips, keep doing what works. See if you can tick at least one of the activities you have listed in the right-hand grey box on your page before we meet again. Do remember, it's normal to have doubts and have some setbacks at times of adjustment and change, be patient, making new connections and settling after your friend has left may take time. Find your bravery, notice what works and be open to what comes your way.'*

Extension activity: You might consider setting up a role play encouraging the child/ren to practice top tips #1 and #2 from the grey box on the left-hand side of their page. Gauge the best way to do this according to your child/ren. A simple way would be to pair up the children, if you are supporting one child be their partner. Choose who will be asking questions and who will be answering. The friendly questioner (not forgetting to smile) asks questions to uncover three interesting things about their partner and writes these down.

Facilitator's top tip: You may like to give some examples of questions to ask or elicit these form the child/ren before they begin. Examples may include: What do you like to do at the weekends? What's your favourite food? What kind of music do you like? Where would you like to travel? Name one thing you can't live without? What's the strangest dream you have ever had?

When they have got their three things, the questioner stops asking questions and reflects the three interesting things back to the person they were finding out about. You may like to give a simple script, something like: 'I'm not going to ask anything else now. I have three things written down about you that are interesting. I'm going tell you the three things now. The first is …, the second is … and the third is …. Did I get that right?' Swap over.

***

Page title: What's in and out of my control?

Page no: 23.

Page rationale: This page helps to understand what can and can't be controlled. Trying to take charge of things outside of one's control can leave people feeling anxious, overwhelmed, and unable to cope well. This negatively impacts wellbeing.

Page visual:

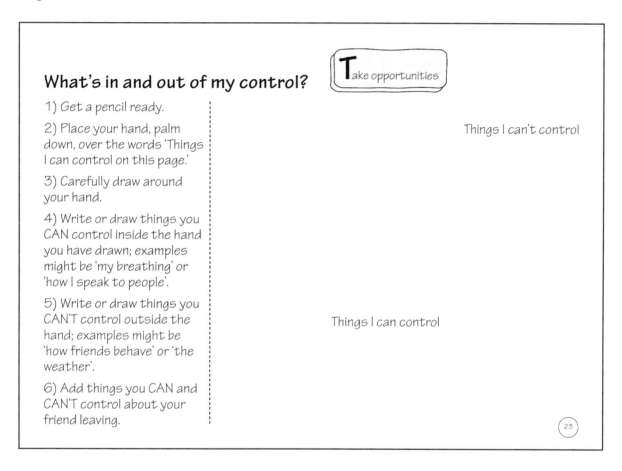

Materials needed: Each child needs: pen, pencil, rubber, sharpener, coloured pens/pencils, activity book. Optional: timer.

Setting the scene: You may say, '*At times of change things can feel out of control. If you spend time trying to influence things that are not yours to control, it can make you feel anxious and upset. Making a choice to focus on what you can control helps you to cope better with change.*'

Completing the activity:

1) You may say, *'The hand exercise on this page will help you understand things you can control and things you can't.'*

2) Guide the child/ren through each of the steps by reading through 1), 2), and 3) on the left of page 23. As you do this you might like to gather examples from the child/ren, in addition to those listed on the page.

Facilitator's top tip: If the child/ren find drawing around their hand difficult, help them out, or ask another child to assist them if you are in a group setting.

3) If time permits, offer the 'What I can control exercise,' below which asks the child/ren to stretch their hand out their hand, palm facing up, and by using their index finger of the other hand keep track by counting through each of the fingers on their outstretched hand, counting five things they are in control of.

Facilitator's top tip: To add a little humour you might like to ask the child/ren to choose their favourite hand.

4) This exercise can be done silently or aloud. Get them to take a big, deep breath at the beginning and end. Encourage them to start each example with 'I can control....':

What I can control exercise:

~Deep breath

'I can control *my feelings.'*

'I can control *my thoughts.'*

'I can control *what I do.'*

'I can control *what I say.'*

'I can control *my breathing.'*

~Deep Breath~

Facilitator's top tip: If time permits, you may ask the children other things they could say instead of the five examples you used.

Closure: You may say, *"It's helpful to remember; 'If it's in your hands you can control it, if not let it go.' If you feel overwhelmed by something, count five things on your hand that you can control. Don't forget your two big, deep breaths at the beginning and end."*

Extension Activity: You may like to try the activity below.

Pipe cleaner and pebble activity:

1) Give each child a pipe cleaner, time two minutes in which they are invited to create something with it.
2) Get the child/ren to share what they have made.
3) You might say '*Great creativity, you changed the pipe cleaner into something, you had control of it, is that right?*'
4) Ask the students to place their pipe cleaner creation to one side.
5) Next, give the child/ren a pebble, rock, or marble. Ask them to create the same thing with the rock that they created with the pipe cleaner. They will most likely respond with 'what?', 'huh?', 'I can't!' Ask them to explain what's different about this challenge.
6) You may say, '*You can't change the rock. You don't have control over what shape it is. Some problems are like the pipe cleaners – we have control over them and can change them. Some problems are like rocks – we don't have control over them.*'
7) Collect in the pipe cleaner and rocks or allow the child/ren to keep hold of them to remind them about what they learned in this exercise.

***

Page title: Appreciating strengths.

Page no: 24.

Page rationale: Knowing and acknowledging one's strengths boosts self-esteem. When we appreciate our positive character traits, we feel more confident and capable. This lifts wellbeing and allows us to be the best version of ourselves. This page introduces the idea of focusing on strengths and builds strength-based vocabulary.

Page visual:

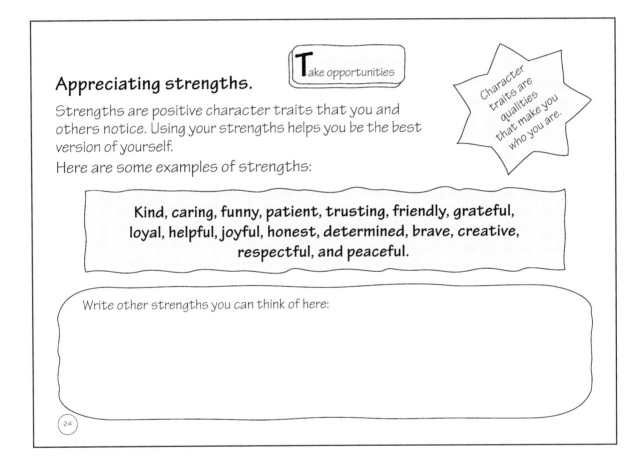

Materials needed: Each child needs: pen, pencil, rubber, sharpener, coloured pens/pencils, activity book.

Setting the scene: You may say, *'On this page we are going to learn about strengths. Strengths are positive character traits you and others notice. Character traits are qualities that make you who you are. Using your strengths helps you be the best version of yourself and boosts wellbeing.'*

Facilitator's top tip: Pages 24 and 25 lend themselves to being delivered in the same session.

Completing the activity:

1) Read through the examples of strengths listed on the page in the grey box.
2) Invite the child/ren to add others they can think of in the box at the bottom of the page.
3) Give each child a blank piece of paper, invite them to write their name at the top. If you are working with one child create one for you as well. If you are in a group setting each child should have a piece of paper with their name on.
4) You may say, *'This activity invites you to write the strengths of the person whose name is on the paper.'*
5) You can facilitate this by swapping papers around the group (or between you if you are supporting one child) or sticking the paper to the persons back whose name is on the paper. The children write the strengths they notice about the person whose name is on the sheet.
6) At the end of the activity, invite the child whose name is on the paper to add a strength they appreciate in themselves to their own paper.
7) Invite child/ren to read through their list. You may like to ask, *'Which strength do you think you have lots of?'* Ask them to share and give an example of a time they showed their chosen strength.

Facilitator's top tip: The child/ren will need their list created in this session for the activity on the next page.

Closure: You may say, *'The cool thing about strengths is that they are always within you, ready to help you be the best version of yourself.'*

Extension Activity: Ask the child/ren to notice times they use their strengths and when they notice strengths in others over the next few days.

***

Page title: Star strengths.

Page no: 25.

Page rationale: This page invites acknowledgement of strengths and encourages the child/ren to think about them in relation to change. We all have signature strengths (these are character traits we find easy to practise and show others) and growth strengths (those we can grow more if we need to call upon them for certain situations). The activities presented promote reflection on these in relation to 'staying well.'

Page visual:

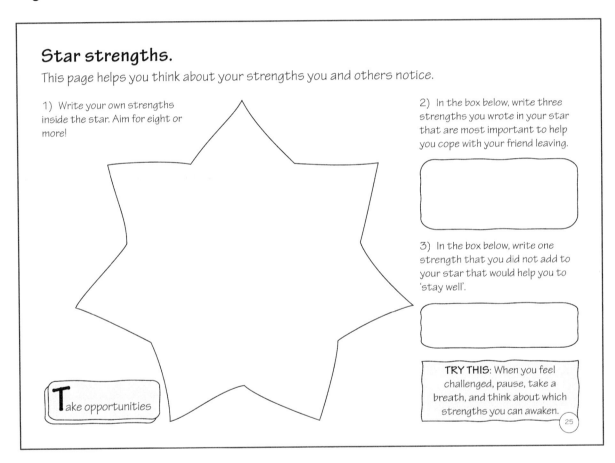

Star strengths.

This page helps you think about your strengths you and others notice.

1) Write your own strengths inside the star. Aim for eight or more!

2) In the box below, write three strengths you wrote in your star that are most important to help you cope with your friend leaving.

3) In the box below, write one strength that you did not add to your star that would help you to 'stay well'.

TRY THIS: When you feel challenged, pause, take a breath, and think about which strengths you can awaken.

Take opportunities

25

Materials needed: Each child needs: pen, pencil, rubber, sharpener, coloured pens/pencils, activity book, personal strength list from page 24's activity.

Setting the scene: You may say, *'This page carries on from the last, you are going to keep thinking about your strengths.'*

Completing the activity:

1) Begin by telling the child/ren they need their strength list generated from the last page's activity.
2) Transfer the list to this page, writing the strengths inside the star.
3) Invite them to add any others they think should be included.
4) You may say, *'The strengths you have written inside your star can be called your "signature strengths," these are strengths that are easy for you to find and others notice you showing them often.'*
5) Next, move to 2) on the page, invite the child/ren to choose three of their signature strengths they wrote in their body outline that will help them cope with their friend leaving. Ask them to write them in the box.
6) You may say, *'We also have growth strengths, these are strengths that are harder to find, they don't come as naturally as your signature strengths. At times of change, awakening your growth strengths might help you cope better. Look at task number 3) on your page, can you think of a strength you didn't add to your body outline but one that would help you 'stay well?''*

Facilitator's top tip: You might share a larger strength list with the child/ren for 6) above.

7) Invite the child/ren to add their growth strength to the box underneath 3) on their page.
8) Find a way for the children to share discoveries. If you are supporting one child, be curious about what they have written in the star and the two boxes. You may ask what made them choose their three strengths they wrote in box 2). You may ask what they need to do more or less of to develop the strengths they wrote in box 3). In a group setting you might like to offer this prompt for each child to speak aloud; 'My three signature strengths that will help me cope with my friend leaving are _____, my growth strength that will help me 'stay well' is _____.'

Closure: You may say, *'Now you've got to know your strengths it's time to start noticing yourself using them. You can think of your strengths as your superpowers you take everywhere you go. When you feel challenged, pause take a breath and think about what strengths you can awaken to help you in that moment.'*

***

Page title: Staying Well podium.

Page no: 26.

Page rationale: This closure and integration activity helps children reflect on what stood out for them from the *Staying Well Activity Book*. It helps pull out pertinent learning and cements engagement with the text.

Page visual:

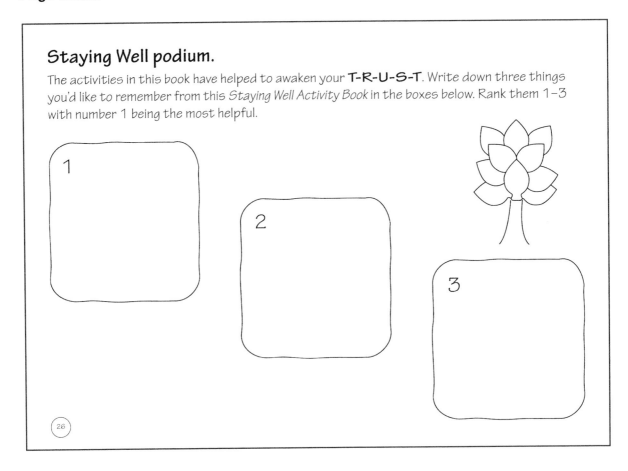

Materials needed: Each child needs: pen, pencil, rubber, sharpener, coloured pens/pencils, activity book.

Setting the scene: You may say, *'As we draw closer to the end of the book, you are going to recall what you'd most like to remember.'* It's a bit like finishing a sports event, you might have seen a podium where the best competitors stand at the end. Maybe you've stood on one of these yourself? This page invites you to place on your podium the most important things you want to remember from this activity book.'*

Completing the activity:

1) Offer the child/ren a summary of things you have covered in the *Staying Well Activity Book*.

Facilitator's top tip: You may ask the children to close their eyes as you recount things covered in your time together. This may help them recall what's been important for them.

2) Ask the child/ren to identify three things they'd like to remember and rank them 1–3, number 1 being the most important, and write them on their podium in the respective boxes. You may like to offer scrap paper for them to make their rough list first, or use the brain dump page (page 33) at the back of the *Staying Well Activity Book*.

3) Find a way for sharing of podiums.

Closure: You may say, '*Everyone's podium is different, just like every person and their journey is different. Thank you for thinking so carefully about yours and what you'd like to remember from the* Staying Well Activity Book.'

***

Page title: Make a Glitter Jar.

Page no: 27.

Page rationale: This page helps the child make their own glitter jar. Using this jar provides a regulatory, visual-sensory experience that helps the child connect with the present moment. Practiced often, the use of this jar can teach the child to activate the part of their nervous system which triggers a relaxation response. It is a great self-regulation tool for the child to add to their coping repertoire.

Page visual:

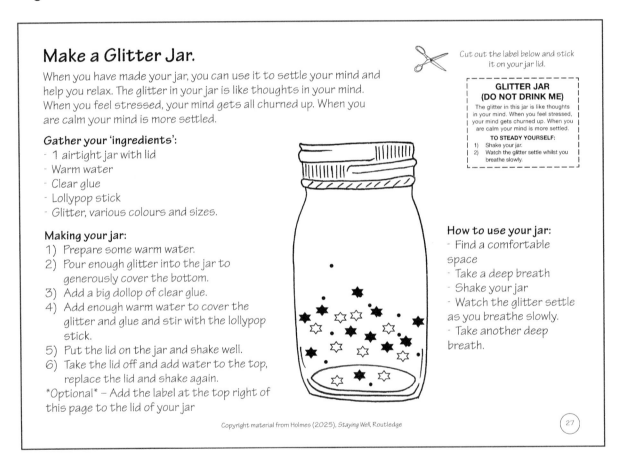

Make a Glitter Jar.

When you have made your jar, you can use it to settle your mind and help you relax. The glitter in your jar is like thoughts in your mind. When you feel stressed, your mind gets all churned up. When you are calm your mind is more settled.

Gather your 'ingredients':
- 1 airtight jar with lid
- Warm water
- Clear glue
- Lollypop stick
- Glitter, various colours and sizes.

Making your jar:
1) Prepare some warm water.
2) Pour enough glitter into the jar to generously cover the bottom.
3) Add a big dollop of clear glue.
4) Add enough warm water to cover the glitter and glue and stir with the lollypop stick.
5) Put the lid on the jar and shake well.
6) Take the lid off and add water to the top, replace the lid and shake again.
Optional – Add the label at the top right of this page to the lid of your jar

Cut out the label below and stick it on your jar lid.

GLITTER JAR (DO NOT DRINK ME)
The glitter in this jar is like thoughts in your mind. When you feel stressed, your mind gets churned up. When you are calm your mind is more settled.
TO STEADY YOURSELF:
1) Shake your jar.
2) Watch the glitter settle whilst you breathe slowly.

How to use your jar:
- Find a comfortable space
- Take a deep breath
- Shake your jar
- Watch the glitter settle as you breathe slowly.
- Take another deep breath.

Copyright material from Holmes (2025), *Staying Well*, Routledge

27

Materials needed: Each child needs: activity book, one plastic airtight jar with lid, warm water, clear glue, lollypop stick, glitter of various colours and size. Optional: label for lid that can be downloaded from the *Staying Well Activity Book Support Material*.

Facilitator's top tip: Please note that for safety', a plastic jar is recommended. Glass jars are not a safe option for young children as they are easily smashed.

Setting the scene: You may say, '*Today, you are going to make your very own glitter jar. This is something you can use to help you settle your mind and relax.*'

Completing the activity:

1) Ensure the child/ren have the items they need to create their jar.

Facilitator's top tip: Consider having a pre-made glitter jar for the child/ren to see as an example before they begin.

2) Guide the child/ren through the instructions under 'Making your jar' on page 27 of the *Staying Well Activity Book*.

Facilitator's top tip: Have lid labels printed and ready if you choose to use them.

3) Before you guide the child/ren through 'How to use your jar,' instructions ask them to choose one word to describe how their mind and body feels – give an example of your own, e.g. 'My mind feels busy, my body feels heavy.' There is no right or wrong. Challenge the child/ren to stick to one word.
4) Now, guide the child/ren through the 'How to use your jar' instructions, at a slow pace.
5) Repeat 3) above. You might like to reflect on their answers by highlighting (if appropriate), '*Sounds like your glitter jar has helped your body and mind relax.*'

Closure: You may say, '*The glitter in your jar is like thoughts in your mind. When you feel stressed, your mind gets all churned up. When you are steadier your thoughts are more settled. If you found using your glitter jar helpful it might be something that you add to your coping strategies. I encourage you to practice shaking your jar, watching the glitter settle while you breathe slowly. You might like to try this when big feelings arrive once you have practiced it a few times.*'

Extension activity: If time permits, you might like to guide them through the 'How to use your jar,' instructions again and include a slow countdown from 10 to 1 as they watch the glitter settle.

***

Page title: Make a Coping Spinner.

Page no: 29.

Page rationale: This playful integration activity brings together regulation strategies shared in the *Staying Well Activity Book*. Making the spinner encourages the child to identify the most helpful coping strategies and reminds them they can make good choices for themselves in moments of overwhelm.

Page visual:

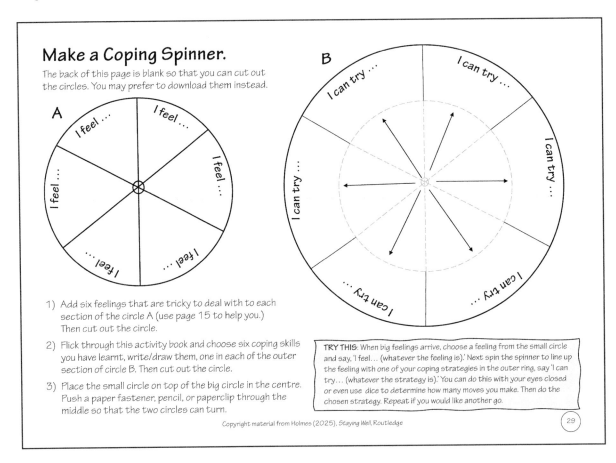

Make a Coping Spinner.

The back of this page is blank so that you can cut out the circles. You may prefer to download them instead.

A

I feel …
I feel …
I feel …
I feel …
I feel …
I feel …

B

I can try …
I can try …
I can try …
I can try …
I can try …
I can try …

1) Add six feelings that are tricky to deal with to each section of the circle A (use page 15 to help you.) Then cut out the circle.

2) Flick through this activity book and choose six coping skills you have learnt, write/draw them, one in each of the outer section of circle B. Then cut out the circle.

3) Place the small circle on top of the big circle in the centre. Push a paper fastener, pencil, or paperclip through the middle so that the two circles can turn.

TRY THIS: When big feelings arrive, choose a feeling from the small circle and say, 'I feel… (whatever the feeling is).' Next spin the spinner to line up the feeling with one of your coping strategies in the outer ring, say 'I can try… (whatever the strategy is).' You can do this with your eyes closed or even use dice to determine how many moves you make. Then do the chosen strategy. Repeat if you would like another go.

Copyright material from Holmes (2025), *Staying Well*, Routledge

29

Materials needed: Each child needs: pen, pencil, rubber, sharpener, scissors, coloured pens/pencils, activity book, scrap paper, and paper fastener (or equivalent).

Setting the scene: Ask the child/ren if they are ready to start making their 'Coping Spinner' You may say, *'When it's finished this spinner can be used for a bit of fun and at times when you feel stressed, it will help you choose a strategy to boost wellbeing when you need it.'*

Facilitator's top tip: As facilitator, keep the instructions on page 29 to hand. It may help to have a completed spinner to show the child/ren to help visualise what they are creating. You may choose to demonstrate the cutting, writing, and fastening procedures with a blank spinner, feel free to download the spinner from the *Staying Well Activity Book Support Material*. You may offer the child/ren the downloaded version or ask them to cut out the spinner directly from their activity books. Printing the spinner onto card helps it be more robust.

Completing the activity:

1) You may say, *'Let's begin by choosing six feelings that can be difficult to deal with. You might like to turn back to page 15 to help with this. Remember everyone is unique and will choose different feelings.'*

Facilitator's top tip: You may like to provide a list of feelings for the child/ren to read.

2) You may say, *'Write your six feelings, one in each section of circle A, on the left of your page.'*

Facilitator's top tip: Some children may prefer to draw pictures, rather than write their feelings and strategies, offer this option if you think it helpful.

3) Ask the child/ren to cut out circle A, and place it on the desk in front of them, some children might need some help cutting the circle out.

Facilitator's top tip: In a group setting you might like to get one child who is working quickly to share their six feelings out loud to help those who may be struggling. You may also use your demonstration example, if you have one, for the same purpose.

4) Invite the child/ren to identify six ways of coping they have learnt from the *Staying Well Activity Book*. Encourage them to flick through the pages to decide what these are. Offer as much guidance as needed.

5) Ask the child/ren to make a list of these on scrap paper, their page, or the brain-dump page (page 33).

Facilitator's top tip: In a group setting you might like to get one child who is working quicker than others to share their six strategies out loud to help those who may be struggling. You may also use your demonstration example, if you have one, for the same purpose.

6) When they have their six coping strategies, ask them to write one in each outer section of circle B, where it says 'I can try…'.

7) Ask the child/ren to cut out circle B, and place it on the desk in front of them, some children might need some help with cutting the circle out.

8) Ask the children to place circle A on top of circle B.

9) Assist, as necessary, with attaching the paper fastener through the centre of the two circles.

10) Read the child/ren the TRY THIS: instructions in the grey box, bottom-right. Use your demonstration example if you have one.

11) Invite the child/ren to have a go.

Closure: You may say, '*So, now you have your 'Coping Spinner' to select a coping strategy at a time when you need it. I look forward to hearing about times it helped you.*'

***

Page title: Awards Ceremony.

Page no: 31.

Page rationale: This closure and integration activity invites the child/ren to reflect on their experience with the *Staying Well Activity Book*. It helps pull out pertinent learning and appreciate efforts of engagement with the material.

Page visual:

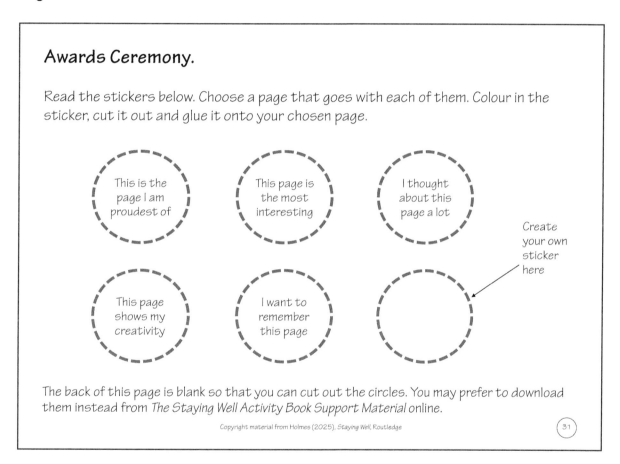

Materials needed: Each child needs: pen, pencil, rubber, sharpener, glue, coloured pens/pencils, activity book.

Setting the scene: You may say. *'You worked hard to complete the pages of the* Staying Well Activity Book. *Now, it's time to give some self-appreciation, by giving yourself six awards.'*

Completing the activity:

1) Invite the children to read through the awards on the page silently or you may choose to read them aloud.
2) Ask the children to colour in each of the circles on their page. Let them know that these are going to be stuck into their book.
3) Invite them to write an additional award they would like to give themselves in the blank circle if they wish.
4) Next, ask the child/ren to cut out the stickers and place them in front of them.
5) Invite them to choose a sticker, match it to their chosen page and stick it in. Repeat with the remaining five stickers.
6) Ask the child/ren to show you, or a partner which sticker they placed on which page and say as little or as much as they would like about that.

Facilitator's top tip: Assit the child/ren as necessary with cutting out the stickers.

Closure: You may say, *'Notice how it feels to acknowledge your hard work, it's been great to see you do this and hear which pages you appreciate most.'*

Congratulate the child/ren on their completion of the pages of this activity book. Let them know you hope their learnings will help them adjust during this period of change when their friend is leaving.

A big well done to you too for supporting the child/ren journey through the *Staying Well Activity Book*.

***

Page title: Brain-dump page.

Page no: 33.

Page rationale: This page is a versatile space for the child/ren to make notes and/or plan. Facilitators are encouraged to use this page as they see fit.

Page visual:

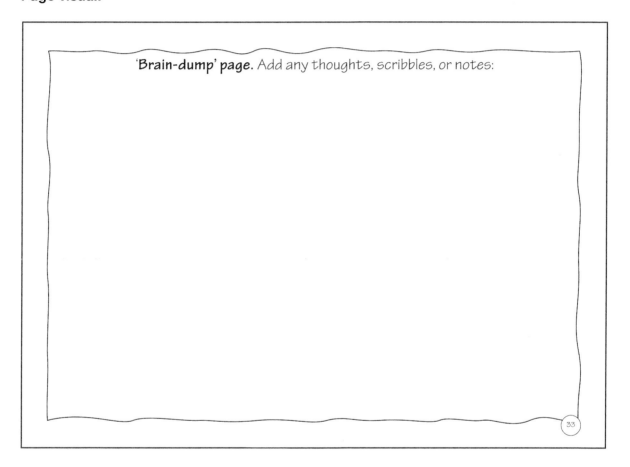

***

Bibliography

Clifford, M.A., 2018. *Your guide to forest bathing: Experience the healing power of nature*. Newburyport, MA, USA: Conari Press.

Levine, P.A., 1997. *Waking the tiger: Healing trauma: The innate capacity to transform overwhelming experiences*. Berkeley, CA, USA: North Atlantic Books.

Mahler, K., 2019. *The interoception curriculum: A step-by-step framework for developing mindful self-regulation*. Hershey, PA, USA: Kelly Mahler.

Neff, K., 2011. *Self-Compassion: The proven power of being kind to yourself*. New York, NY, USA: HarperCollins Publishers.

Ota, D.W., 2014. *Safe passage how mobility affects people & what international schools should do about it*. London, UK: Summertime Publishing.

Pollock, D.C., Van Reken, R.E., and Pollock, M.V., 2017. *Third culture kids: Growing up among worlds*. Boston, MA, USA: Nicholas Brealey Publishing.

Seligman, M.E.P., 2002. *Authentic Happiness: Using the new positive psychology to realize your potential for lasting fulfilment*. London, UK: Nicholas Brealey Publishing.

Seligman, M.E.P., 2012. *Flourish: A visionary new understanding of happiness and well-being*. New York, NY, USA: Atria Paperback.

Siegel, D.J. and Bryson, T.P., 2012. *The whole-brain child: 12 revolutionary strategies to nurture your child's developing mind*. New York, NY, USA: Bantam Books.

Index